# HEALING HEARTS

*Shatterproof*

True inspirational stories waiting to be gifted.

JEANINE LEBLANC

Tellwell Talent
www.tellwell.ca

Unbreakable Heart bead on front cover
available at www.greengirlstudios.com

ISBN
978-0-2288-5028-1 (Paperback)
978-0-2288-5027-4 (eBook)

I'm splitting my dedication into healing-heart pie.
The first cut is to you, just you. Specifically,
to the child-self you've carried inside.
Next cut is for Erin Usciski; #74 Stitch-Rip-Her.
The rest is for my mom, who I was never meant to keep,
but carry for a lifetime.

# TABLE OF CONTENTS

Rushton Luoma grew up on a farm in rural Alberta and currently lives in Calgary with two fur kids. A varied career has led to well-rounded interests and skills. First and foremost, Rush loves camping. She can usually be found at her permanent campsite during the summer when work allows. With an attached private golf course, golf has become an obsession. Collecting found golf balls has too, just ask her friends. Rushton recently completed a screenplay and has a patent-pending in her name. Rush invites you to join her journey and challenges you to 'finish' yours.

# FINISHING ME

## *By Rushton Luoma*

One of the first things I can remember being mad about during my childhood was when I had to start wearing a shirt because I was a girl. I was probably around seven or eight years old. I also hated wearing dresses. For my fourteenth birthday, I remember getting a new ten-speed bike and being furious to the point of tears that it was a 'girl's' bike.

What I loved was growing up on a farm in the 1960s with my older brother and two younger sisters. Early in my childhood, my mother was in a wheelchair, so my siblings and I ran the household and learned the value of hard work. Dad was a seed grower for the federal government, which meant he was instrumental in test growing new seed varieties in different climates and soil conditions. As we kids got older, we operated every type of equipment in the fields. We grew up with religion as well—not the radical type, just the average, rural Albertan, Bible-belt kind.

After school sports weren't usually an option, so our entertainment was riding our bicycles all over the yard and playing in the coulees and hay bale forts. We played with all the baby goats, calves, and kittens, and they all had names. As we got older, we had horses, then 4H horse club, and later, we graduated to dirt bikes. With a square mile attached to the home place, we had ample room to play and grow.

In later years, as my breasts were developing, I forever fought with having to wear a bra. I wore larger and larger shirts to help hide the profile. I always felt I was more than a tomboy, but didn't know how to explain it. I just hated my breasts, and I hated my given name. In fact, back in those days, there was nothing to even explain. Being something other than a boy or a girl wasn't an option. In later years, I also discovered where I was in the hierarchy of things—the farm came first, my brother came second, and in the mentality of a farmer, the girls were last. I always wanted to farm, but dad never gave me that opportunity. I believe that was because I was a girl. Growing up mostly left me confused and uncomfortable about who I was and who I was supposed to be.

After high school, I became an emergency medical technician and worked on ambulances for twelve years. I was also a medic in the Canadian Armed Forces (Reserves) at the same time. I still didn't like my chest, but I liked the work well enough. One of my highlights as an EMT was volunteering for the 1988 Calgary Winter Olympics. As a 24 year old, being able to work behind the scenes at such a high-calibre event was incredible.

Around 1986, I started playing women's ice hockey and discovered I was attracted to women. After some months of struggle with my religious upbringing and how I felt about myself, I had no doubt. I liked women. I had one eight-year relationship and a couple of shorter ones. Other than that, my relationship status ranged from severely happy for a short time to heartbroken and single.

In 1993, still unhappy with my chest, I had a breast reduction. I didn't really know what to expect, but they were smaller, so I guess I was happy. One thing I didn't know was that unless they remove all the breast tissue, they grow back. Over time, I had to start wearing and buying larger bras again. For a long time, I accepted it as the thorn in my side that I just had to live with. I went through periods of great depression about life in general and my sexuality. Confused about who I was and not knowing how to feel any differently, I started drinking and smoking heavily.

After watching drag shows for years, I took the leap and became a drag king. I loved the stage. There, I could be someone else for the night. Sometimes it made me feel like I was someone, other times I felt so low. Back then, kings were pretty rare in Calgary. For many years, I struggled as the only active king in a large charity fundraising organization. I had great support from the queens, but limited peer support from my women friends. I'm not sure why; they just didn't like drag.

Not being able to share the one thing I loved led to more periods of depression. I felt inadequate because my breasts obviously weren't in-line with the look I was attempting to achieve. As a drag king, I had several acquaintances who'd had top surgery, but I didn't talk to them or ask for advice. Now I feel like I didn't use the resources that were available to me. At the time, I think I just assumed they were all transitioning, which wasn't what I wanted. I just didn't want breasts.

Somewhere around 2014, a friend had a second breast reduction. I hadn't realized a person could have another one. I also didn't know what other options I could ask for, so when I saw the new surgeon in 2015, I just said I wanted to be as small as possible. After I woke up from the surgery, I didn't look or feel very flat. I remember thinking, "There better be a lot of swelling there." Several weeks post op, it was apparent I still had my problem of breasts. I felt I wasn't just a woman, but a woman who liked women, but didn't like her own breasts. I really didn't know how to identify anymore.

Discussing my displeasure with friends over drinks, as you do, I learned that one friend was having the female to male transgender top surgery and had already had a breast reduction. I finally realized that this could be a possibility for me, too. Although I wouldn't say I was ecstatic or excited, my quest was renewed. I was still full of self-doubt from having two reductions without the desired results, so I wasn't confident this would work either. Most of all, I just desperately wanted to feel comfortable in my own skin, and that was enough to make me willing to try again.

In 2017, I again began the referral process to get a surgeon. This time I knew I needed to have a psychiatrist sign off for me, so I saw one. He signed it on the first day. On top of that, he said I was to continue with ongoing appointments and prescribed me some medication for bi-polar disorder. While on the medication, I gained over fifty pounds and it did nothing to ease my sense of discomfort. Eventually, I asked my family doctor what she thought about his diagnosis and treatment. She was shocked he'd put me on those meds. After reading a letter from this psychiatrist filled with misinformation, there was no doubt I was to stop seeing him and get weaned off the meds. This didn't hold me back from my vision of finishing me.

In August of 2019, a surgeon finally contacted me. Our newly elected provincial government had changed some requirements and created new hoops to jump through for a breast reduction, so the process to get approval for Provincial Health Care to cover the surgery was challenging. First, I had to get a psychiatrist's signature on a new form. Since I wasn't his patient anymore, the psychiatrist I'd seen refused to sign. I researched his name and found that almost every person who'd reviewed him said they were diagnosed with bi-polar. Glad to be done with him, I struggled through the stress of finding a new psychiatrist. I also did a lot of other research and even had some excellent counselling from the Skipping Stone Foundation in Calgary. That helped me to understand all the terminology, as well as my own experience. I finally understood what I was really feeling and how to put it in words. I was also armed with answers for questions like, "Why aren't you on hormones?" or "Why would you want top surgery but not full transition?" but the new psychiatrist didn't even ask. He listened to me and signed off right then and there. I was grateful.

This new understanding of who I was felt like an opportunity to change my name on social media. At some point, I may change it legally, but for now I'm not prepared to answer questions from work colleagues and people who don't need really to know. I changed my name to Rushton, and never in recent memory have I been more relieved. Finally, a name that felt like it belonged to and made sense for me.

2019 became my year to finish some big projects and ideas. I'd thought up many inventions over the years, and finally followed through on one. Now I have a patent pending on one. Twenty-plus years before, I'd also started a screenplay, but never did anything with it. I finally finished it and even entered it in a couple of screenwriting contests in early 2020. Although I didn't place, I was encouraged with the feedback from the evaluators. One of my highest marks was for character development, creating people who were "believable and richly rendered." I'd done that, and it felt good.

Although the top surgery was delayed twice, I was actually at peace with waiting. Of course, I couldn't do anything about it anyway. The worst part of being rescheduled is that my countdown kept restarting. Three more work days, two more work days, then—boom—fourteen more days. Twice.

In February 2020, my bi-lateral mastectomy for female to male top surgery finally happened, and the hospital staff and surgeon were amazing. When the admitting nurse asked if I had a preferred name, at first I said no. But then I decided to do something for myself. After a minute or so, I said, "Actually I do," so she put it on my chart and from that moment on, to them, I was Rush. Without a second of judgment, I was accepted one hundred percent as Rushton. I can't tell you how satisfying that felt. I wasn't scared or nervous. I knew this was where I was meant to be.

When they walked me into the operating room, at first there was a problem with the controls on the table. All I could think was, "Seriously? I'm so close."

They resolved the problem quickly and the anaesthesiologist went through everything that would be happening to me. Her calm voice and explanations reinforced that I was in the right place.

Just over three months post-op, I'm happy and comfortable in my body, an experience I've wanted for my whole life. I've lost most of the weight I gained from taking that carelessly prescribed medicine. Still a bit to go, but isn't there always? I'm excitedly discovering I love the ease of going out and not having to wear a jacket or baggy sweatshirt. For too many years, those were my security blankets. Since I don't have to hide my chest profile, I stand up straight now, too, not hunched over. Now, because my outside matches my inside, I have more confidence in everything I do.

In the months leading up to my top surgery, I finally learned to use the resources available to me. I realized that for about the last ten years, I've identified as asexual and that, although I don't want to be a man, I also prefer to identify as male. I believe this may be where the attraction to women came from, and maybe not because I was a lesbian. I finally understood that I'm kind of in-between a few identities. I was gender dysphoric without even knowing what it was. Through work with various counsellors, I've learned to like and be happy with just myself. I have great friends, but I prefer to be alone romantically.

Most of my adult life, I've made decisions based on what others have wanted me to do. For years, I kept a name and maintained a gender identity that felt true to everyone but me. I didn't farm because I wasn't supposed to be a farmer. For a while, I took the wrong medication because a psychiatrist told me to. Now I've learned to—and continue to—make myself stand up for me and do the things I want to do. Sometimes it's difficult as I could upset a friend or family member, but I need to take care of myself first. If I don't, I know I'll let myself be brought down again.

I often wonder how the life a person is born into can affect them long term. I wonder about my name, my gender, and my own insecurities. How much did those things affect what I chose for a career? How much did they affect my depressions? My confidence and comfort within my body? I know people who, to me, have exciting careers and beautiful partners. I know people with names that suit them as well as supportive families, and I wonder where I'd be if I had all that from the start. Would I have been happy? Would it have changed my sense of self-worth? Would I have had the perfect life and career too?

I don't have answers to all of these questions, but I do know that my life will continue to be a learning and growing experience. For some time now, a poem by Walter D. Wintle has been my strength. In the last stanza, he writes, "Life's battles don't always go to the stronger or faster man, but sooner or later the man who wins is the man who thinks he can."

I know I can't get back those 'shoulda, coulda, woulda' moments. But, if someone doesn't support who I am, they're not for me. I deserve more than discomfort, confusion, and someone else's expectations, and only I can create my future with no regrets. The moral of my story is that I need to have courage to take control of what I can change in my life. Which is exactly what I'm doing.

Charise Thompson lives on a small acreage in Wyoming with her husband of thirty-seven years and their rescued four-legged children. Semi-retired, Charise continues her work as a minister, victim advocate, and counsellor, also facilitating two support groups she founded in 1994. 2020 is her 11th year as a roller derby coach, a sport she fell in love with and played back in the 1970s. Charise holds numerous poetry awards, including an International Poetry Award, and continues to write in her spare time. Charise and her husband share five grown children, ten grandchildren, and three great-grandchildren. They love to travel and hope to do more of it in the future.

# RAPE: THE LONG ROAD BACK

### By Charise Thompson

I lie still in the stench of the drainage ditch they'd thrown me in, watching it turn red with my blood. Terrified that they would return, I want to die. Life had already been hard. At just twenty-four years old, I'd known child abuse, molestation, drug addiction, leaving my home country at sixteen, domestic violence, and now a most horrific and brutal gang rape. Hadn't I been through enough?

I knew my body was badly broken, my skull fractured, my teeth broken and missing. I had stab wounds bleeding profusely and my insides no longer inside me. The pain was excruciating, and I kept blacking out. These six men had beat and repeatedly raped me—done both with a tire iron. They'd drilled holes in my ankles and tried to hang me like an animal. They'd dragged me behind their truck before running over me and savagely beating me some more.

It was November 1981, the American Thanksgiving weekend when my son and I had gone to Corpus Christi, Texas, to spend time with mom. On the return home to Laredo, I had a tire blow. I got out to change it and was just finishing when a truck pulled off and a man approached offering help. I thanked him, but declined, and heard him walk away. The door slammed and I could hear the truck on the gravel. Then something moved and I turned to look down the barrel of a gun. I couldn't breathe. Panic rose inside me as I was shoved into the back of the white crew cab. We drove off, leaving my son, Jason, locked in the car.

I thought about my poor mother about to lose her fourth child. I'd be the third in a year and my heart broke for her. My brother Craig died the year before, and my other brother Roy six months earlier. I closed my eyes and waited for death. All I could see was the smiling face of my five-year-old son alone in the car on the side of the road and I wouldn't, couldn't, leave him out there. I had to get help to him, no matter what.

I gathered every ounce of strength in me and crawled out of that ditch on broken bones, wrists still tied together. Every foot was more painful than the one before. I had to keep stopping. I'd dig a little deeper and crawl a little further before I'd black out again. I crawled for hours on a dirt path before I saw a small house. I couldn't scream, so I banged on the door. A sleepy man and his wife answered. They were horrified by my appearance. They carried me into the house and covered me with a blanket. He left to call authorities and returned with the ranch owners, who offered comfort until the ambulance arrived.

My jaw was hanging on one side. I couldn't speak but made motions. The police got a pen and paper and, after a series of scribbles, I got through to where my son was. I prayed he would be there and alive. They did quick patches and loaded me into the ambulance. I don't remember much, just lights and voices and busy people all around me. I remember talking to my brother and telling him I wanted to go with him, but he said, "No Reecie, you have to go back. You still have so much to do". Then he was gone. I remember a lady coming in to say that they had my son and that he was fine. He was safe with my friends I'd given a contact number for. I'd never known that intensity of relief! I knew that no matter what happened to me, he'd be taken care of.

After thirty-one units of blood, four months in the hospital, in-patient rehab, and many surgeries, I was going home to our apartment—my safe space—and James was coming home! Unfortunately, my safe place no longer felt safe and I felt terrified all the time. I thought I saw their faces in every crowd, so I isolated and withdrew. Then one day that familiar white truck was on the street in front of my apartment with two of the men inside. I decided to move back to Corpus as soon as I could pack. I knew I could find an apartment there.

Because my mother had lost two sons already, she was hanging on by a thread. I was terrified she'd go after them herself, since she was a cop, so I let her believe the account of an accident that my friends told her when I had been unable to call. It was a few months later when I told my mom the truth. At first, she was upset I hadn't told her sooner, but agreed that she might not have reacted well at the time.

I started working for Chris, a friend in Corpus, at a private mailing center. Never could I have imagined the blessing that he would become in my life. I struggled terribly with nightmares, panic attacks, and numbing fear, so I finally went to the Crisis Center for help. At times, I just wanted to block it out, but knew I had to remember in order to deal and heal. Slowly and steadily I worked through the terror and life became easier.

I became a volunteer at the Crises Center. One day the counselor wanted me to talk with a woman who had been gang-raped at college. I did, and it was through that experience that I learned my greatest healing would be in helping others to transition from victim to survivor. As bad as the experience was, it gave me insight and experience that no one else could have. I understood that I could help victims who had been feeling alone and scared!

After a year of working together, Chris and I dated casually. He was the kindest, most patient man I'd ever known, though there was no shortage of issues that we struggled to deal with. I was emotional and would alternate between pulling him close and pushing him away. Some days I couldn't stand to be touched and others I didn't want to even talk, but he hung in there. A year later, we married in a small ceremony and, shortly after, he retired from the U.S. Navy.

I ended up needing an emergency hysterectomy due to complications from the attack two years before. Afterwards I got sick, though testing didn't show anything that made sense physically. The doctor suggested I see a psychiatrist. I was devastated after everything I'd been through and disgusted that he could think the issue was in my head.

In 1989, we moved from Texas to Wyoming and I started as a victim advocate for Safehouse. After completing their training, I worked in the office, the shelter, the twenty-four-hour crisis line, community work, and helped with new advocate training. I was well—truly well—and I wanted to help others to find their way.

I also sought medical help again in 1989, and biopsies named it Hepatitis C. Now my symptoms made sense! In 1990, I did the first human trials with Interferon. The treatment caused rapid acceleration of the disease and liver damage, followed by a series of strokes. One massive stroke put me in a wheelchair and doctors were sure I'd never get out of it, but I refused to believe them and continued to work hard on my rehabilitation. During this time, my ability to work with Safehouse was limited. So, in 1995, I started online support groups for people with Hepatitis C and sexual assault. I also became an ordained minister. My desire to help others was now a burning passion and a need within me. Then, in 2009, I finally worked my way out of that wheelchair which opened a new world for me.

In 2010, I went with a friend to check out roller derby, since I'd played in the '70s. I was adopted as "team mom" that same night. A few months later, I became their coach and have been ever since. I'd been a counselor and started a women's group for addicts, but it wasn't enough. In roller derby, I had the opportunity to help so many more people, in so many ways. The sport thrived. A dozen teams then became hundreds and then thousands around the world.

I counsel when that's what they need. I do weddings, baptisms, funerals, commitment ceremonies, and anything else I'm asked to do. But most of all, I listen. I listen to people tell their story and, when right, I offer suggestions or resources in their area where they can get local help. Just by hearing their stories, I am able to fill a void for many victims.

Six years ago, I woke one morning and felt different. It was like a light had come on and I knew I had to do more to speak up and spread the word to reach more people. I published my story on Facebook, complete with a picture the authorities had taken in the hospital sometime shortly after the night I fought so hard for our lives. I heard from people everywhere, some applauding my strength, others telling me their stories. I knew we had to raise awareness and bring sexual assault out of the darkness and into the light. I had to speak out about how wrong the stigma is. I knew this much too well. One officer had asked me, "What did I do to make them so mad?" And a doctor said that "I wasn't going to make it, but it was just as well . . . who would want me now?" Like I had done something wrong or was to blame for the sadistic rape and attack. I had to speak out and I keep speaking at every opportunity.

Every year I repost when the anniversary of my first post comes up. Year after year, I hear painful stories from dozens of women, men and youth. Some find the courage to share their story for the very first time! To be of further help, I keep updated lists of resources in each state in hopes to give everyone a starting place in their healing process.

I completed a six-month drug trial of Harvoni in 2013 and then did six months of Sovaldi/Ribavirin. Following the treatment, I did another Hepatitis C treatment, but it was a complete failure. Then, in 2017, I went into spontaneous remission. Doctors really don't have the answers to how that happens. I saw it as a miracle and a sign that I was on the right path. So now I keep pushing forward to bring attention to sexual assault victims and show them that what they feel is normal. The course they take is theirs and I am here for them along the way.

2020 felt like a whirlwind as both The Sun and the Daily Mail in the UK published my story. I heard from magazines, Dr. Phil's producers, as well as other shows and newspapers that wanted to share my story. Committing to a podcast on recovery, this anthology, and an international magazine has helped me to realize the potential of my purpose. I am blessed to be able to share my story so widely and help so many.

The dozens who responded to my Facebook post became hundreds as it went around the world. I spend countless hours now on the phone, in chats, messenger, or online groups. I will not turn anyone away. If they have a story to tell, I want to listen and support them however I can. It's my goal to help as many as is humanly possible move from victim to survivor! People say my courage gives them the strength to report sexual assaults or tell their families their stories. Knowing this, I will continue my mission and my ministry. I will travel to where I'm needed, as much as finances allow. I will help as many people as I can, any way I can. There is life after rape . . . a joyous and worthwhile life!

I AM A SURVIVOR AND A SURVIVOR I WILL ALWAYS BE!

Brittany comes from a small farm village called Stirling, found in Ontario, Canada. She is the loving mother of two children, a boy and a girl. Aside from being a marine biologist, Brittany lives out her passion as an artist and paints as her profession. She also loves Norse mythology, history, and astronomy. Brittany's hobbies include collecting Viking artifacts and taking pictures of Saturn with her telescope. When she was twenty-nine, Brittany was diagnosed with major depressive disorder after becoming very ill. The past two years of her life have been spent navigating this diagnosis. She hopes to write fantasy novels one day, as J. R. R. Tolkien inspired her at a very young age. Currently she stays home with her kids, painting art for her shop, while her husband works at sea.

# LET GO OR DIE

## *By Brittany Goodfellow*

I was raised in an illusion. An outside observer would have seen a pristine home in the suburbs and a family consisting of two well-behaved daughters. However, I was the daughter from my father's first marriage, and a smear on the image of perfection his new wife wanted to maintain.

My father was prone to spontaneous episodes of rage and blamed me for his misery. I still remember the case of soda being thrown at my head while he accused me of being just like my "selfish mother." He raised me after my mother abandoned me to move in with a man, who she had met online two hours away.

As a hypersensitive child, my emotions would sometimes overwhelm me. I could look at a field of grass and feel the essence of my spirit or watch a bird in the sky and understand the meaning of life. I rarely spoke and cried often. My hypersensitivity permeated into every area of my life and I cherished it immensely, though my parents did not. I was raised to believe that emotions were weak; in order to succeed in life, I had to toughen up.

The restrictive way in which I was raised only exacerbated my introverted nature. I was regularly grounded for not giving a strong enough handshake or being too quiet at social events.

They aggressively tried to instill confidence into me by shaming me for being shy, and I often found myself living more in my internal world than in theirs to escape it. Their world consisted of military-level obedience and superficial extraversion. I became afraid to ask permission to go to the movies or to a dance. I felt like a prisoner held in a cage.

Becoming rebellious with age as a way of protesting the oppressive nature in which I was raised, I decided to throw a party while they were at work when I was fourteen. When they came home to find beer bottles and teenagers cluttering their perfect lawn, I was exiled to live with my mother.

Things took a turn for the worse after I transferred schools. I became a drug addict at fifteen, anorexic at sixteen, and would often run away from home only to be brought home by the police. I dropped out of high school twice. My mother was suffering through an abusive relationship she could not escape, and I would often hear them fight. When the fights became physical, she would scream and beg me to help her. My father rarely spoke to me for three years during this time.

Drugs led me to an eccentric, exciting boy with bipolar disorder and alcoholism. Despite his problems, he accepted me as I was, and we decided to move to the East coast together so I could attend university. I thought I could save him. Unfortunately, his illness consumed him. He spent more than two years physically and emotionally abusing me. He stole my tuition to buy drugs, destroyed my personal belongings, and was arrested multiple times for beating me. I knew I had to save enough money to escape him, so I was forced to sell my body to a middle-aged store owner in secret for five hundred dollars. I took the money and moved out only to have him track me down and threaten to kill me and then himself. My roommate called the cops and he was arrested. I never saw him again. Despite being free of him, a primal fear began taking control of my life and I started having panic attacks and major depressive episodes.

It was when my father called to tell me he had a life-threatening type of liver cancer two years later that my mind began to experience bouts of madness. Unresolved emotions between us had instilled a severe anxiety disorder consisting of sleep paralysis, nightmares, panic attacks, and trips to the hospital. I was unable to hold a job or maintain social relationships because of my mental health. I nearly dropped out of university, and began self-medicating with alcohol to lessen the anxiety that was taking over my life. I received a phone call from a family member during this time telling me to fly home immediately.

My father was dying. At the peak of my new illness, I flew across the country to be with him in his final three days of life. On his deathbed, he vomited blood as his eyes rolled backwards, and I found myself with post-traumatic stress disorder and a permeating fear of death for years to come. I spent those days apologizing for disappointing him. He forgave me, yet apologized for nothing.

It was only when I met my current husband that things started to change for the better. I had every intention of ending my life before the age of twenty-five, but upon meeting him it was as if the universe itself had whispered to me, "I have not abandoned you." At a human rights protest, I noticed an incredibly handsome young man up on the stage giving a powerful speech to the audience.

Something pushed me to introduce myself, and upon meeting we were instantly drawn to one another. Things progressed very quickly as we realized we were kindred spirits in a chaotic world. We had a child together when I was twenty-three, and by the time I was twenty-nine, I thought I was ready to have another. Little did I know that by not actively working on my trauma I was predisposing my brain to a condition I never knew existed, a condition so terrifying it would change my life forever.

Just weeks after giving birth to our second child, a daughter, I began experiencing what I now refer to as "the dark wave." I'd ridden the waves of clinical anxiety for years, but this was not anxiety. In the span of two days, I went from functioning to feeling as though I had entered another dimension. I was vomiting daily, sometimes so violently my throat would bleed. My muscles ceased working properly because I could barely stand upright. Waves of chemical terror descended upon me as my brain was no longer working properly, and I began isolating myself to the basement. I could no longer care for my own children. My husband took over completely as I deteriorated into the abyss. Years of abuse, trauma, and hormone shifts had launched me into an illness that is experienced by just one in one thousand women that give birth—postpartum psychosis.

The doctors treated me as though my depression was situational and would resolve with antidepressants. When I took them, I experienced a worsening of my symptoms. I began seeing shadow figures and having violent nightmares about suicide, as well as delusions that I was going to die. I went to the hospital five times, only to be turned away each time and told to continue taking the drugs which were making my symptoms significantly worse. Days were spent pacing in circles around my house, sobbing hysterically, and screaming to my husband that I was going to die of my own fright. I could not sit still to read a book or watch a movie, and every second of every day was spent in utter agony.

For nearly four months, I fought relentlessly to control what I was experiencing, and tried to hide my psychotic symptoms as I fell deeper into the episode. My sense of time became warped. Each minute felt like an hour as I paced frantically in a state of severe agitation. I had always associated depression to sadness, but I was not sad—I was terrified.

I visited counselors weekly, none of whom could tell me what was happening to me. When I asked my psychiatrist if I would ever be well again, she replied, "I don't know, I'm not a fortune teller."

The words "let go or die" devoured me as I sat on the brink of oblivion. I knew I had to be hospitalized, but allowing this required me to release control and I resisted. After several months of unrelenting distress, I could no longer keep fighting.

As I held the phone in my hand I knew I was at the major crossroad of my life, and if I did not call 911 I would die. In that moment, I chose life. I wanted to save my life for the sake of my husband and children, even if it meant facing my worst nightmare. With shaking hands, I dialed and knew that it would be the final time I would go to the hospital. Instead of resisting the inevitable, I finally allowed myself to fall headfirst into the unknown and called an ambulance. I was admitted as an inpatient and escorted to my room in the psychiatric ward where I would remain for nine days. I felt a shift within my mind upon entering the ward, a sensation of release. I had to be put on antipsychotics immediately to stop the episode which I now understand was a deadly combination of mania, melancholic depression, and psychosis. Once the agitation stopped, my appetite slowly returned, and I began venturing out of my room. The release from the grip of the episode was unimaginable. I could feel my brain turning back on.

I began to experience emotionless lulls, as if my brain were rebooting back to factory settings, followed by spurts of emotions.

I met friends in the psychiatric ward who lead me on small adventures around the hospital and instilled a sense of excitement into me which began to override the fear from within. We would meet in the television room and sing songs, sharing our stories of madness, bonding in our shared experience of having been to 'that place' within the human psyche. I began to see them as veterans of depression and was inspired by their strength. There was no need to control my symptoms in the ward for they were as sick as I was, and for the first time I knew I could fully let go.

Upon remission from the episode, I spent the next year seeking answers as to what happened to me. I remembered one common thought amidst the delusions during the time I was ill, and that was, "let go, or die". I knew that if I did not take the steps necessary to face the trauma and let go of control, one day I would face another episode of major depression.

Today, I am a survivor of what I see as "the war within the mind." I survived a trip to the deepest and darkest trenches of the human psyche. Taking inspiration from Vincent Van Gogh— who also experienced the turbulent seas of madness—I picked up my paint brushes and found peace in the act of creating art. I knew that postpartum psychosis had ignited in me a deeper ability to express myself through painting as my art took on a deeper quality. I then realized that even the darkest experiences can lead to beautiful things. I also began practicing cognitive behavioral therapy and finally understanding that mental illness is not a weakness, as my father would have implied. Rather, it is an illness that can be helped with therapy of the mind just as physiotherapy helps a broken leg.

In the act of letting go and allowing myself to be helped, I faced my deepest fear of all— the loss of control. I learned that allowing panic attacks to happen without resistance strips their power away. To survive trauma is an incredible sign of strength, and the realization of that strength became more addictive than the fear that had once possessed me. Traumatic experiences had taught me that I had to constantly maintain control because my internal world was always so out of control. By letting go, I accepted my experiences without resistance, and the path of least resistance ended up leading me to emotional freedom.

Instead of trying to control my mental health by fighting it as an enemy, I learned to accept my limitations and see my experiences as learning tools rather than obstacles. It was in this shift in perception that I learned the importance of letting go. I was taught by my father to believe that hypersensitivity was a character flaw, but it was that same sensitivity that lead me to the beauty of creativity, and the realization of the artist within me.

The darkness of postpartum psychosis birthed a profound awareness of my own bad habits that predispose me to further depression. I learned to channel my distress into *what I can do to feel better,* rather than indulging in the cycle of habitual thought patterns that lead back to depression and anxiety. Ultimately, though, I let go—and in letting go, I finally felt free.

Jennifer Omoth was born and raised in Edmonton, Alberta. She attended Camosun College in Victoria, B.C., and graduated with a cooking apprenticeship in the early '90s. Over the next twelve years, Jennifer served her dishes for a few esteemed inner-city restaurants. After having her daughter in 2005, she decided to move her career to food distribution. For the last decade, Jennifer has been employed with one of North America's major suppliers.

Through the years, Jennifer experienced lots of hard living, good times, and many difficult lessons. It wasn't always negative, with many life experiences adding to her unique, fun-loving, and colourful personality.

Edmonton drew her back in 2007 so she could live in the same city as her parents. Her choice to move allowed for a wonderful relationship with her folks and her daughter. Now, Jennifer finds few dull moments as she jumps life's hurdles while raising her fifteen-year-old. Time couldn't be better spent with her family and fiancé.

# NEVER LOWER YOUR STANDARDS

### *By Jennifer Omoth*

In the early 2000s, I frequented the Ship & Anchor pub in Calgary, Alberta, looking for a way to fill the emptiness I felt inside. Daily, I lowered my standards and made horrible decisions, whether that was drinking too much alcohol or having a one-night stand with the wrong guy. I'd struggled for much of my life with self-love, and the only relationship I'd had was an abusive one. Somehow, I decided that the void in my heart could only be filled by a man, so I became infatuated with the idea of having another boyfriend.

At the time, I had good friends I loved and who loved me. Often, I'd cook up big feasts for everyone. An avid snowboarder, I was at the mountain almost every weekend, lapping up the fresh air and beautiful scenery. That never felt like enough, and neither did I.

On one of my nights at the Ship & Anchor, I met a guy. I was in awe of his style, looks, and personality. Despite warnings from other people, we moved fast and found a place to live together on the top story of a house. I ignored his shady reputation with drugs, stealing, and lying. Since I was also edgy and not bothered by much, he seemed like a good fit for me. Blinded by my longing for a relationship, I didn't really care about rumors that came my way.

Around the same time, I found my cat, Bart. This seven-week-old kitten became my everything. In the top story apartment, Bart was noticeably stressed by my relationship choice. I knew my boyfriend wasn't being good to Bart and, although this raised a flag, I still couldn't leave the relationship behind.

The boyfriend and I had a few things in common. We both loved alcohol, smoking dope, and dabbling in cocaine. It wasn't long before we found ourselves lost in the darkness of a crack addiction, and I became a functioning crack head. Every day, I managed to make it into my full-time job as a professional cook. Despite how some mornings felt, I never phoned in sick. What money my boyfriend and I had left after bills was spent on drugs, cigarettes, and alcohol. When the well ran dry, we became an ugly sort of train wreck. When the well was full, it overflowed. Many of our friends who worked in the oil patch loved to hang at our place. They would lie to their spouses and show up with wads of cash. We all had a safe place to get high until the wee hours of the morning. Our addictions became hard-core, and I knew in my heart that I was no longer one of the living.

Eventually the boyfriend and I were evicted. After that, we found it tough to keep a place. Consequences for our bad choices eventually brought us to the Motel Village ghetto, across from the C-Train station and McMahon Stadium. It was the most disgusting room I'd ever occupied. Bloody hork ran down the walls, and stained polyester sheets covered the mattress. Homeless men lived below us, and the stench of stale beer from the empties that sat in their shopping carts engulfed our room. I woke up crying and went to bed crying. This was the absolute lowest I'd ever felt. I was stunned by what I had become.

We stayed in Motel Village for about a week, maybe ten days. Every day, I brought myself to work, knowing full well that I was deteriorating, and my appearance was changing. I'd lost weight and appeared gaunt and exhausted. My period didn't come for a couple of months, and I chalked it up to all the stress. I kept my parents in the dark about my lifestyle. When we spoke, I lied or just left out details. Many of my friends knew the relationship I was in was poison from the start, but I wasn't willing to end it. Instead, I put up a wall between me and the people who loved me. When I found my rock bottom, the only way to cope was to get high again.

Our newfound walk-up apartment wasn't great, but provided the space to keep up with our brutal habits. This pad became the place to get high—not only for our oilfield friends, but also for different drug dealers. The bills didn't get paid, and we had no groceries. By some sort of miracle, we didn't get evicted. While I was at work and when we were out of money, the boyfriend would go through my belongings and look for anything of value to pawn off for drug cash. Unemployed, he spent his days making deals with stolen items and ripping people off.

At night, while we got high, a police helicopter often circled our apartment building and area. The bright helicopter lights would shine straight through our window, which made all of us paranoid. Looking back, I figure we were under surveillance because our dealer, there with us, was most likely wanted. Somehow, I continued to barely survive through this horrible lifestyle and toxic relationship. I hated him, but I also hated myself. Through it all, I learned that you get what you give. I was as much a part of the toxicity as he was.

One unusually sober Sunday night at home, my life managed to take a deeper dive. We were watching TV, and I felt the need to pee. In the bathroom, I found that I was bleeding heavily. Terrified, I wondered what damage I'd done to myself. With a bath towel cradled between my legs, we left for the hospital.

By the time we made it the Foothills Medical Centre emergency room, I could feel the effects of losing tremendous amounts of blood. I remembered that I'd missed several periods, and that I'd blown it off. The denial of a drug addict. Now, I assumed I was having a miscarriage. Traumatized, I cried harder than I ever had and blamed myself for the choices that led me here. When a doctor came by to assess me, he first relayed that I was still pregnant. I cried and said that there was no way I could be pregnant with the amount of blood I'd lost. After a second inspection, the doctor realized that what he'd seen was a baseball sized fibroid, which had caused me to miscarry my baby. I felt that my crack addiction, not the fibroid, was the killer. I was a mess.

Standing at my bedside, the boyfriend kept turning his head away from me. He said he was having trouble looking at my face, particularly my eyes, because they were almost swollen shut from crying. I hated him more than ever. He had no compassion for me and what I'd just been through, or even for himself for the loss of his baby.

I needed to have the fibroid tumor removed, and leading up to the surgery, I had to have a Lupron Depot injection once a month, for three months. Health Care didn't cover the costly injections, so my dad kindly offered his support. Embarrassed, I didn't tell my parents about the miscarriage, or anything else. In retrospect, I wonder how all of these health issues didn't make me get my head out of my ass, but they didn't. I had the fibroid c-sectioned out of me, and heartbroken at the loss of the baby, I carried on, back to crack.

As time went on, I knew that my miscarriage was a blessing in disguise. With the amount of drugs, alcohol, and cigarettes I was consuming, that child would have been very sick. Also, I was nowhere near ready to be a parent, especially not with that man.

At the time, I couldn't see clearly or love myself enough to get out of the relationship, so I did what I needed to stay in it. To get more dope, I sold anything I had with value. Anytime through the night I could also run to Money Mart for a pay day loan. The emptiness I thought I'd fill with a boyfriend just turned into more emptiness, on the inside and out.

While waiting for my surgery, I lost my job. Afterwards, I found a new one, cooking at a little café on 8th street, near the Mountain Equipment Co-op Store. Ironic, since snowboarding was now only a distant memory. My shifts at the café were long, from 7:30 in the morning to 3:30 in the afternoon. Regularly exhausted, I fell asleep on a few occasions while standing on the kitchen line. I was noticeably unsafe at work, and I know my co-workers wondered what the hell was wrong with me. Still, I managed to hold my job and show up to work every day.

One of the few mornings that I wasn't sleep deprived and hurting, karma found me again. While upstairs in the little loft used for office space and dry storage, I gathered up what I thought I'd cook for lunch. With both arms full of cans and soup stock, I proceeded down the Dutch-style staircase, which meant steep stairs with tight turns. On the fourth step, my kitchen clog rolled over the edge, and my foot launched me down the stairs. I must have been in shock when I hopped up to our raised kitchen and accepted money for a coffee from a customer. The customer realized I was badly damaged and stayed with me until my manager arrived. X-rays taken at the 8th Avenue Health Clinic showed a brutal break to my right ankle. I would need a plate and twelve screws to put it back in place. Fortunately, Worker's Compensation would cover it.

This injury was yet another beautiful blessing in a dark disguise. My suffering body needed healing, and I was wiped out from living with addiction. The boyfriend wasn't willing or able to take care of me as I recovered, and I knew I couldn't stay where I was. Even after that terrible fall, I was somehow still alive. I longed for a life in which I loved myself, and I was ready to make healthy choices. It was time for a visit home and to push the reset button. My loving parents drove from Edmonton to Calgary to gather me up. While in Edmonton, I finally slept and ate well, and my ankle was healing. For two weeks, my parents took care of me, and I was able to take care of myself in a new way. I got strong enough to return to Calgary and get back to Bart, who was still in the apartment with the boyfriend.

Unfortunately, when I walked through the door of the crack shack I'd called home, I found the place destroyed. The cops had raided it while I was away. Another push of the reset button. I finally decided to leave the boyfriend and get out. I needed to start packing my belongings, but I was pretty much useless with the cast on my right leg. Mentally, I also felt ruined. I just sat on the couch and cried in disbelief. I reached out to my most solid friends, who despite the walls I'd put up between us, showed up with bells on to get me out of the hell I was in. I was beyond grateful, and I got myself and my cat a lovely little bachelor apartment.

To let my ankle fully heal, I couldn't return to work for about six months. I had to work with a physiotherapist to learn to walk properly again. Unfortunately, quitting drugs wasn't as easy as leaving my boyfriend behind in the wrecked apartment. Also, although I'd reconnected with my old friends, I still was keeping company with people who weren't good for me.

A new friend of mine was in a jam and needed to move out of her house and leave her boyfriend too. She pleaded with me to be her roommate. I agreed and moved out of my lovely apartment, right back into my crack addiction. Bart was still with me, but hadn't been doing well. I was worried. I found out he had kidney failure and had to put him down. On top of that, my new roommate was ripping me off. What she did to me wasn't what woke me up. Instead, it was watching her life go down the drain. I could see what had happened to me happening to her, and that's when I gave my head a big shake. I wasn't going to let myself go down the drain again. I quit using drugs and moved out.

Six months later, I got pregnant by a casual lover, and I fell in love with my unborn baby. Suddenly, I understood how to love unconditionally, and although I'm not a religious person, this baby felt like my saviour. A miracle in my life. Because I was worried about miscarrying again, I had an early ultra-sound. I found out that my pregnancy was rolling along nicely, and my baby was doing well.

Now I had the time and clarity to walk the hallways in my head. I had a lot of forgiving to do with myself—for stupidity and bad calls and all the hurt I'd caused. After healing from my fall and now in this pregnancy, my mental health demanded my attention. For the first time in a long time, I looked after myself, doing necessary soul searching and listening to a lot of Jack Johnson's mellow music. I focused my everything on getting ready for a new life, and my world changed forever when I gave birth to my beautiful and healthy baby girl, Ella.

When Ella was two, we moved to Edmonton to live closer to my parents. I joined roller derby and worked hard at becoming athletic. I also found a new profession in food supplies, and I love taking care of my customers.

Since Ella came into my life, I no longer lower my standards, and I know I don't need a man to make me feel complete. I make healthy choices and, just as my true friends did for me, I help out anyone in a spot, whenever I can. I try my best to be true to myself, and I see a psychologist as a way of taking care of me. Ella is now fifteen years old—an amazing kid and honour student—and I have a wonderful, healthy-choice fiancé who I love so much.

I may always carry anxieties associated with the darkness I've experienced, but I can make it through knowing that my heart is genuine, my standards are high, and I am one very proud mom.

Carole is a retired schoolteacher who now lives on the Eastern Shore. She has four grown children and three grandchildren. Carole enjoys writing, gardening, and reading as many books as possible! Above all, she loves to go walking in the mornings with her chocolate lab, Hunter, and then spend the rest of the day spoiling her two rescue doggies, Trapper and Tigger. In these most difficult times, she remembers her dear grandmother and her stories of suffering and sacrificing through two world wars and the Depression.

Dear reader, it is as if words of wisdom are whispering on the winds:

"Be still and know that I am God."
Psalm 46:10

# DON'T YOU TRUST ME

## By Carole Chandler

I sailed through my first two pregnancies. Okay, there were red flags, but I ignored them. My first baby was a preemie. Henri survived, asthma and heart murmur aside. And yes, scarcely a year later, I did spot with my second child, but after a day, the bleeding stopped. My worry evaporated when Jean arrived, a husky, healthy seven-pounder.

I took it all for granted, and so ten months later, I plunged into round three, just expecting to waltz through.

I had planned to revise my lesson plans on Labour Day, because I was excited to hit the classroom for another year of teaching. At dawn, when I got up to pee, my whole body froze with shock. Red . . . everywhere . . . on the floor tiles, the toilet paper, and my pyjamas. Never has a colour terrified me like that red on white. Hands trembling, I called my doctor.

"Stay calm. Go to bed. Call me at noon."

*Is that it?!*, I thought. *That's the best you can do? Just sit tight and wait?*

A painful childhood had filled me with anger, impatience, and distrust. The years ahead would force me to face these demons. By lunchtime, the bleeding had stopped. At suppertime, still nothing. The next day, all was well. I rested, got the green light from my doc, and wobbled back to my boisterous grade tens at Cole Harbour High. Everything was alright, I convinced myself.

Thanksgiving arrived. I played with the kids, never realizing what lie ahead. But Tuesday morning, in that nasty school bathroom, reality hit hard. Bright blotches of blood had stained my skirt. Grabbing my coat to hide my embarrassment, then running to the office, I felt as if an icy bucket of water had hit my face. Hours later, I stared at the fuzzy ultrasound. The nurse whispered:

"The baby is gone. Your body has reabsorbed it."

That was the most bizarre thing I had ever heard. I returned to school in two days, but spent months grieving. Each evening, I would walk the roads along the seaside talking to God, telling Him I wasn't mad, just hurting. There were no support groups for miscarriage back then. Therapy became an empty ritual. The priest who had baptized me glared and pronounced:

"Had you nursed your baby longer as God intended, you would have never gotten pregnant so soon. This is your punishment for disobeying Him."

His cruelty bruised my soul. People say the damndest crap.

"It's for the best."

"It's not so bad that it can't be worse."

"You can always have more."

I turned bitter. Oh, sure. Why not? Let's just try to hatch another one! And so I did, four months later. Then at thirteen weeks along, sobbing in a filthy service station restroom, I held my baby in my hands, placenta and the whole gory mess. Where was God? Why wouldn't my body work like it should? My mother's harsh words flooded back in a rush: "Carole, you are textbook brilliant, but life stupid. A real dopey dud."

Well, I did have a 'perfect' miscarriage this time, the nurse announced, with no hospital D&C. I drove home, stunned. It was April 30th. Determined to not be a dud, I got pregnant again by May 18th. My medical team was furious. What in hell was I doing? What was I trying to prove? And to whom?

And by July, I sat with my specialist.

"Tonight will be a long, tough labour. We'll get you to the O.R. tomorrow. Save the pieces of tissue as you pass them, for testing."

Something happens when a woman huddles on a cold hospital floor at three a.m., cradling a tiny arm and leg in her bare hands, that hellish red dotting the white tiles and more red running down her legs. Innocence is lost, faith is shattered. I ring for a nurse. No one comes for over an hour. By then, I'm clutching the toilet for support, staring at a miniature umbilical cord that has just flowed out in a gush of blood.

My mind snapped. I have never been the same. Hours later, I lay waiting for surgery, craving comfort. A hug. A hand to hold. The hospital was a zoo. Nurses were running in and out, busy, busy, busy. Having no idea where to find the peace I so desperately needed, I pulled out the Bible from the night stand.

I made a vow, then and there: When I get out of this damn place, I will read the Bible from cover to cover. Never again will I not know where to look.

I have kept that promise for thirty years.

But the suffering continued. I endured painful fertility workups. Once, they accidently put me into a room with eleven women about to attend their final prenatal class. I stared at all the bulging bellies, then bolted. A nurse found me, curled up in some hallway somewhere and summoned a psychologist. I was definitely not okay. After months of prodding and poking, the fertility tests showed nothing. No conclusions, no hope. People were smoking, drinking, and partying, yet still popping out babies while I had lain in bed, crept around on tiptoes, trying not to miscarry. By November, my doctors shrugged and told me to try again, someday. I was so frustrated.

That Christmas Eve, I stared at the blue line in the white square. Pregnant. No way! I drove to the drugstore for a second test. Positive. I bought another kit and headed home. I hung the stockings, tucked my boys into bed, and stared into space. I prayed hard. Was God my friend or my enemy? I wasn't sure. Dawn arrived. In a surreal dream, I watched everyone open gifts, I cooked dinner, went to church, and then sneaked downstairs to do the third test. Clearly preggo. I called my specialist.

"Be in my office tomorrow morning, ASAP."

So there I was, eyeball to eyeball with a man who had only bad news.

"Carole, six pregnancies in five years, three of them miscarriages this year! That makes you a spontaneous aborter, giving this pregnancy a fifty-fifty chance. You have Rh-negative blood. Plus, the fertility tests increase the risks considerably."

I left, filled with artificial hormones and a heavy heart.

Clutching my Bible, I bargained with God that if He let this baby live, it would be my last.

I was already dog tired in January when a lousy flu virus hit. I soldiered on until February 21st. Henri's cake was baked and his presents all wrapped. Promising to get him early from daycare, I walked into class that morning, hoping for peace and quiet. Then I went to the bathroom. Droplets of red peppered my white panties. No! Please God! Not on my son's birthday. How cruel can You get?

By 10:05 that morning, I was spread out on an ultrasound table, on the bottom floor of the same hospital where, three years before I had been on the top floor giving birth to Henri at 10:06 a.m.

The technician ran the scan, and then abruptly left. A doctor swept in. I lay numb.

"Is my baby dead?"

"Your baby is fine. You have a complication. Placenta previa. The placenta is across the bottom of your uterus and it can tear as the baby grows. It's bed rest or you could both bleed to death."

"When do I start that?"

"You just did. Ten minutes ago."

For six months, I laid on the couch, trying to manage with two kids. Man, it was hard. We cuddled, watched T.V., and Henri became my gofer. I couldn't have coped without him. And God.

Bible study became my refuge. As I grew bigger through the summer, I drew comfort from the Psalms of King David—a man whose journey of suffering paralleled my own.

But my doctors kept warning me. The odds jumped to ninety-ten that I would lose the baby because of placenta previa.

"When will the baby be safe? At thirty weeks? Thirty-six?"

"We'll feel safe when he's in your arms. That's the reality."

I sunk into depression.

On September 3rd, Labour Day, my son arrived. Blue. There was dead silence in the delivery room.

"What's going on?" I cried out.

More silence. Doctors rushing around, whirring noises, then a feeble whimper.

"He's alive," a nurse whispered. "We're putting him in the incubator with oxygen to pinken him up."

Hours later, as I held him tight, I made a vow: *His name is Christien, because he is a gift from Jesus. Every time that I say his name, I'll be thanking Him.*

I took my baby home on a sunny autumn day. But I wasn't well. I was so traumatized that I wouldn't let Christien out of my sight. Flashbacks of gruesome images and nightmares plagued me. More therapy. More prayers. I became convinced that he was going to die.

"Don't you trust me?" The voice whispered to me one night.

"God . . . I just don't know."

Even when Christien turned eight months old, I was still a wreck. One evening, in total despair, I threw myself on the floor and begged God to protect him. That's when I heard, gently but firmly: "Don't worry, I'm watching over this little one."

I still fretted constantly. I tried so hard to believe. I knew in my heart that a divine voice had spoken to me, but I struggled to surrender and accept God's peace.

The cold started up in late November, turning into a bad cough. Christien's little chest heaved with exertion at each breath. I rushed him into the Izaak Walton Killam Hospital for Children at three in the morning, only to be brushed aside by a young resident and sent home. No one told me that Christien had croup and that croup gets worse on the second night. I tore home from school next day. The babysitter stood, rocking the baby. His face had no colour.

"Carole, he's getting worse."

I called the E.R. and as I was speaking to a nurse, she interrupted:

"I can hear him from here, honey. That's really bad croup. Come in immediately. Roll down the windows to get lots of cool air."

I race through Dartmouth, over the bridge, and just hit Robie Street when Christien starts to gasp for air. I turn to look. He's blue.

Suddenly, I hear a deep, male voice saying, "Stop! Get an ambulance, now!"

I swerve into the nearest driveway. It's the same garage where I had my second miscarriage. I'm wearing the same sweater. I skid to a stop and scream:

"Call me an ambulance! Now!"

A mechanic is drinking a Coke. He stares and lowers the can in slow motion. I scream again and he springs to life.

The ride is hellish, with paramedics working on Christien, radios squawking and me thinking, *This is not a dream, this is real! I'm not watching some TV drama that I can click off because it's too intense.*

In the ambulance bay, nurses grab the stretcher, slam it through double doors, and then Christien disappears into the ICU.

"What are You doing? Didn't we have a deal? Didn't You promise to look after him?" I rage at God out there in that void.

*Don't you trust me?* I hear back.

I slump over, totally exhausted.

We were in the hospital for a week. The resident that had blown me off the night before got some serious shit from his superiors. Christien looked like a corpse in his oxygen bubble.

He slowly recovered, but remained frail. I trusted no one, though I reflected on the specialist's words: "Carole, if you hadn't stopped when you did, your son would have died en route. He was in respiratory failure. We had only a few minutes to get him breathing again before cardiac arrest."

But, it wasn't me. Stubborn me would have kept driving. Some force larger than myself had compelled me to stop that fateful day.

And as the pages in my Bible slowly turned over, one by one, filling me with love, so did the months and years of motherhood.

Today, I still worry and go to therapy. Christien is a strong, healthy man now, with his own child. He has followed his passions and chosen 'Nova Scotia's most deadly occupation.' Every time he is out there, fishing on that ocean with the winds howling, my old terrors ignite. My stomach churns. Then I push the pause button on my anxiety.

***Don't you trust me?***

"I guess I do, dear God and dear Jesus. You've brought us both this far and You've been with us all along. You never promised to save me from bad things, just to shelter me when they happen. Hell, if I'm going to trust in anyone, it's gonna be You. I accept Your gift of peace. I can't imagine life any other way.

Prayer for Loss
Miscarriage is a lonely, miserable experience. I am so sorry you are going through this. You have the right to grieve. Please take as long as you need. Above all, be kind and gentle to yourself. May your heart be healed.

Jeanine LeBlanc is a former member of the Canadian Armed Forces, business owner, and roller derby athlete. She is not only 1-0 in the ring of the Canadian Boxing Association but has also come out on top as a co-author in the Canadian bestseller *Sacred Hearts Rising—Finding Your Wings.*

As an empath child, Jeanine cared for several small, broken wild animals. She was drawn to their transparency and innocence and found it difficult to return them to nature. Several years following a childhood filled with struggles of a different kind of survival, Jeanine was forced to undergo a darkened journey back to the heart of the little empath girl she once was.

Now surrounded by forest on Nova Scotia's Eastern Shore, her unique and rustic residence is home to nearly three dozen rescue animals, many of which require high-needs care. Jeanine feeds her creative desires through writing, building her landscape or sculpting on the inside walls of her quaint country home.

# CHANGING TIDES

## By Jeanine LeBlanc

I was just eleven years old on that Canada Day in 1984 when Stoney Beach in Lawrencetown, Nova Scotia, swallowed my mother. The Atlantic Ocean, Tide of Death, stole her soul and changed my every tomorrow. Anything my mother loved, my father had removed from our broken home. Waiting to be exiled from the front lawn of our private military quarters was her favourite living room chair, clothes, and artwork. Days following my mother's drowning, my father travelled to her hometown in Harrisville, New York, to attend her funeral. She went home a hero.

The day her life was devoured by the ocean, my mom announced that we would start collecting our beach toys and packing them up for the near-hour drive home. The sand tunnels we dug throughout the day would soon become part of the sea. My mother disappeared through the sun's light as she made her way toward the ocean water to wash the sand from her suit. Dad packed up our blanket and beach towels while we sat alongside in the sand.

Time passed while we sat looking and waiting for our mom's face to reappear through the crowd. As I looked at each person, their faces began to appear more distant and disconnected. Everyone seemed a part of their own world as ours began to grow uneasy. My energy shifted from that of a playful child to an uneasy, anxious cloud. Our dad had our uncle walk us to our parked van while he disappeared toward the dark sandy edge of the beautiful unknown.

Inside our van, we sat quietly while an ambulance whistled its way toward the tea house perched less than one kilometer at the top of the hill. I watched as the waves rolled in from the wide-open sea and the beach grass danced in the warm summer breeze. Time passed, no word.

Swimmers shouted and laughed while others ran through the shallow water at the ocean's edge. I could feel us as strangers, our two separate worlds held generously together by the cool ocean tide. We were just another face in the crowd. I expected mom would shortly return and give us a detailed story of the emergency. Time passed, still no word. Facing the tea house, we watched the ambulance whistle back down the hill and past our van. Our parents should return now.

Moments later, following the ambulance, we saw a white, full-sized truck. Watching as the truck rolled by, we could see our dad waving through the window of the front passenger seat. Time stood still. It was that one sudden moment when I felt any faith within change to fear. There were just so many people left on the beach that it felt incredible that anything could disrupt our family beach day.

Once at the hospital, our uncle parked, and we quietly sat inside the van for someone, anyone; a sign. Time passed. As the world outside disappeared, suddenly dad exited through the steel door of the hospital building. Our van's side door had been drawn open to allow a breeze to cleanse our intense wonder and fear. His shoulders were strong, and his voice was brave, but his eyes reflected his grieving soul. I felt the awful truth he was not ready to share.

"She's dead, isn't she?" I yelled. Dad didn't need to answer. He hugged us so tight I could finally feel his love.

Over the next few days I saw pictures of our family photo on the front page of different newspapers. "Hero Mom Mourned" was the heading written across one. "I'll lend the province money for lifeguards" says the man who pulled the body from the water. "Woman drowns, girl rescued at Stoney Beach" wrote another. We learned our mom had courageously helped a little girl struggling within a current, then lost her battle to the sea. We were never meant to keep her.

Just a few weeks following our tragedy, I was given a date for major back surgery. I had been diagnosed with Sprengal's deformity, a rare congenital skeletal abnormality where a person has one shoulder blade that sits higher on the back than the other. The deformity is due to failure in early fetal development.

Not knowing how to reconnect with life after our tragedy, I was left emotionally exhausted, terrified, and alone. The day my father dropped me off for the procedure at the IWK Children's Hospital in Halifax, sixty-seven stitches would trail my spine. Visits from my father and siblings were infrequent. I can recall my sister sitting across my recovery room with tears swelling in her eyes. Dad had accused her of being jealous of the attention I was receiving and had been hitting her in the backseat of the car. Even though I needed him, it seemed better that they didn't visit at all.

Our family was granted a grievance posting following mom's death. This means the government would fund our move to Sydney, Cape Breton, to live close to our extended family. In Sydney, my father would have an accounting position at the military radar base.

My stitches were barely healed when we made our drive to Sydney in late August. On arrival, our diminished family stood in front of a tall, old and blue spooky house nestled behind a beaten down garage amongst the rotted trees. An old tire swing dangled through the air from the arm of a careless apple tree. This would be our first taste of public, community living. There was no way of knowing how I was supposed to fit in amongst a neighbourhood of civilian children.

Our father employed a full-time babysitter for his days away at work. By the time school began in September, dad announced that he was dating his old high school flame. He grew angrier toward us while protecting his happy new life from our grieving hearts. The days felt as though our previous life was null and void. We were not permitted to mention our mother. One evening at bedtime, my brother sadly called out from his room: "I miss mom." My sister and I wholeheartedly agreed, "We miss mom too." Dad busted into our bedroom and ripped us from the protective covers of our bunkbed. He hurt us; he physically beat us for our sadness. My father never understood how to connect with our painful energy. He was not comfortable with love, so his anxiety would turn to rage. By December, just six months after our mother drowned, we reluctantly sat in a church and witnessed their vows. All I could think of was how much I missed mom.

When we first met our future stepmom, she was a light to be found in the dark. I remember our first heart-to-heart in the bathroom of that old creepy house. She wanted to be a loving part of our lives and promised to come with the patience to earn it. We understood that she was in no way there to replace our mom. Selfishly, I wanted her there to protect us from our father. I knew he was not about to unmask his rage in her company when he was focused on winning her love. We had a chance to feel safe. But, selflessly, we warned her that night of his anger and that she should think about reconsidering. I recall her saying that she could have quite the temper too. She didn't understand.

She was not like our father.

As you may expect, our dad was unable to keep his true colors hidden. It was shortly after their divorce in 1991 that I dropped out of high school and followed my father's footsteps by enlisting as a cook in the Canadian Armed Forces. At seventeen years old, and for the very first time, I felt he was proud.

During the first year of my military career, I was posted to Calgary, Alberta. It was here where I stepped out of my displaced lesbian closet. I realized quickly that was a door better left bolted. As a result of my courage, I was sexually assaulted by a fellow co-worker. I kept the trauma silent and continued to work alongside the man who violated my being and my plea to stop. All the while, other female co-workers openly cringed with judgement whenever we shared the same space at the mess hall. My performance declined and my light dimmed. I paid a visit to the base padre and then filed a request for my release from the Canadian Armed Forces.

While awaiting release approval, a morning came that my alarm clock malfunctioned. Torn between the fear of impending consequences and the incredible release of breaking free from abuse, judgement, and control, I raced towards work, only to stop partial way. Time stood still. I sat in my car and just cried before turning back toward home. I was officially AWOL.

The consequences for not returning to my abusive government job began by becoming a Wanted Person across Canada. I didn't know what else to do, so I packed to survive in the woods of the Canadian Rocky Mountains.

Nature called me back to freedom and, for a moment, I felt connected and alive.

But I knew this freedom wouldn't last. During a phone call with family, I learned they had been contacted by government officials in Ottawa. After 21 days absent, it was time to stop running. Surrealness was an understatement when I bravely pulled open the door and introduced myself inside the Calgary Military Base Police Station. Officers on shift were familiar with my identity and I could feel their excitement. They proceeded to check me in and lock me up in a video-monitored cell. Humiliated, I was forced to painfully remain standing each day from the moment I woke up until lights out. There was nothing more to do than lean against a wall and try to make some sense of a Bible left behind.

When the day of my court martial arrived, I was given two choices. I could reveal the names of my abusive co-workers or accept my consequences for AWOL. During my court martial, I nervously stood at attention before the judge and my light suddenly blew out. Knowing I would soon have to return to work in the mess hall, I was too scared to vocalize any names. When the verdict came, I was surprised to learn I was being sentenced to prison. Two officers stood by to escort me to the final step in Canada's disciplinary chain.

I marched through the front doors of a two-story concrete prison enclosed with high fencing and barbed wire. My blurred lifeless reflection followed me across the polished flooring down an intense yet silent hallway. I was put into a room with a female guard who demanded I removed my uniform and under garments. Being stripped of clothing and locked outside had been a punishment at our house growing up but removing my clothes as a form of punishment as an adult emptied my soul.

Shortly after, I learned the following privileges I would have as a Stage One Inmate:

- No talking
- No cigarettes
- No visits
- No phone calls
- No TV
- No computer
- No personal effects in cell
- No eye contact
- No sounds in the cell (monitored)
- No walking (fast-paced march only)

Each day began with a 6 a.m. wake up call and ended with mandatory lights out at 9 p.m. Every morning I would have to replace the laces in my footwear they had confiscated the night before. Hours between the days were packed with humiliation and punishment, as well as the duties and drills required to advance to the next stage of sentencing.

After lights out, I stood there in front of the bars of my window and became more aware of human imperfection, gratitude, and forgiveness. The glow of the city lights danced under the winter's night canopy. Time stood still.

Still a teenager, I served my sentence and walked through the exit door of Canada's Military prison. Shortly after returning to my posting, I was granted my request for an honorable release from the Canadian Armed Forces.

On the outside, *the dark* found me vulnerable and lost. Following my father's death in my twenties, I succumbed to numbness through addiction and depression. I suffered with anxiety and shame from the intensities that came with being an addict. I had lost my battle and will to live in the tight grasp of cocaine, crack, alcohol, and gambling. At thirty-four years old, the age my mother's life had ended, I expected to disappear like she had through the crowd of empty faces. I believed this was all that life would ever have for me.

It was during this crash, my empty years, when I felt most desperate. I can visualize myself seated in front of my computer doing searches for my mother's name; for anything related to her. I reached out into an abyss of nothingness in hopes to find a miracle, and carried my pain like it was the only thing I had left of her. It was here that I found a small speck of light drifting in time and space. One of those newspaper articles I had carried through the years, "I'll Lend the Money for Lifeguards," had been written by Lesley Choyce. I found Lesley to be a resident of Lawrencetown and a well-known author. Feeling within a flow, I searched several of his items for some connection. "Death Comes to Stoney Beach" was a short story written inside one of his several books. With certainty, my mother was not the only victim at Stoney. But there I saw the names of both my parents written across pages of this unfamiliar story.

I had learned on that Canada Day weekend in 1984, it was author Lesley Choyce who showed up to carry our mother to shore, while I sat in the sand waiting for her face to reappear. It was Lesley who had kissed her soft lips and begged our Almighty to bring her home as if he was the last to ever love her. After sharing my found treasure with family, I connected with Lesley in a letter to thank him for his courage.

As time passed, I worked hard at healing and recreating my world. Reconnecting with my child-self and carrying her along lightened my load. She was forgiveness, compassion, and empathy. Her bravery forced my every uphill step until I stood at the highest point in front of my X the spot. I became an athlete and worked to escape every addiction. I moved from Edmonton, Alberta, to Nova Scotia's Eastern Shore, just short of an hour from Stoney Beach. Here I found flow, solitude, and self-love. My country home has become a rescue to several wild, sick, and abandoned animals. Because of everything I've learned, I have gratitude for all I can give.

A light can persist through a tunnel of hope. Both Veterans Affairs Canada and the LGBT Canadian Class Action Lawsuit have compensated my claims of suffering assault, harassment, and imprisonment during my career in the Canadian Armed Forces. I have since received a Letter of Apology from the Chief of Defence Staff.

Prolific author Lesley Choyce was born in Riverside, New Jersey, in 1951. He studied at East Carolina University and Livingston College, received a bachelor's of arts from Rutgers University, and has master's degrees in the arts from both Montclair State College and the City University of New York Graduate Centre. Lesley is a Canadian author of over ninety-four books, both fiction and non-fiction, including children's books, young adult novels, and poetry. He teaches in the English department and transition year program at Dalhousie University. He is a year-round surfer and founding member of the 1990's spoken word rock band, The SurfPoets. Choyce also runs Pottersfield Press, a small literary publishing house, and hosted the national TV show *Off The Page* for many years. His books have been translated into Spanish, French, German, and Danish. He has also been awarded the Dartmouth Book Award and the Ann Connor Brimer Award.

# DEATH COMES TO STONEY BEACH

## By Lesley Choyce

J uly 1—Canada Day. I am lying down on my bed in the middle of the afternoon.

Holidays always made me lethargic. The phone rings and I swear, learning that someone is caught in the tidal current of the Lawrencetown River at Stoney Beach and is being sucked to sea. I know there are no lifeguards there, even though its waters are warm and swimmers plentiful.

I jump in my car, drive to the nearest beach, and scream to the lifeguards to follow me to Stoney.

I race on ahead, facts sorting themselves out in my brain. Seconds count. On this rare warm summer day, the beach will be jammed with swimmers from Halifax and Dartmouth. At low tide, the river empties the lake into the sea with a strong, deep channel that comes too close to shore. It's not an undertow, just gravity racing inland waters back to the ocean.

I can't drive fast enough. Traffic is sluggish near the headland with drivers slowing down to look at the blue, clean ocean. I smash on my horn and curse out the window. Finally, I clear the top of the hill and pull into the tea room parking lot, run to the edge of the high dirt cliff, and look down and out to the sea. Nothing. Nearby, beneath me at Stoney Beach, everything looks normal. No one running, no one screaming. The sound of kids laughing lifts high into the air and finds me here, baffled, feeling startlingly alone. Something tells me not to assume too much.

Directly below me, on the loose stones and boulders near the tip of the headland sits a young man on a rock. He looks like he's been swimming. I jump the edge, wearing nothing on my feet but cheap rubber sandals, and slide the loose soil and scree to the shore's edge, a hundred feet down.

"Is there someone out there?" I ask, pointing out to sea. My heart is pounding. I'm already out of breath. The guy shakes his head. I see his pale, ghostly face. He's shivering and hugging his knees.

"I tried," he says to me, groping for his words.

I'm half-hypnotised by the sound of the people having fun so near. So hard to keep convincing myself it's a crisis.

"She's still out there," he says.

"Where?" I ask.

He points a finger. Weighty seconds pass. I can see that the river current snakes close to shore here before it loses its strength and blends with the wide open ocean. I follow its path with my eyes out to sea.

Then I see something. I see her. Face down. I start running over the slippery rocks toward the victim. I fall several times, tearing my legs on sharp barnacles. My sandals fall off and I'm stumbling along in my socks. The water rises toward my chest and I swim. I'm shocked at how warm it is. I was expecting ice, as always. But it's the river sucking warm inland water out of the lake. The sea is so warm that I know that something is very wrong.

The swim is not far, but it is enough to get me into the water twenty or thirty feet deep. I'd lost my lungs long seconds ago on the way down to the headland. Now I cursed myself for being so stupidly out of shape. I'm gulping for air and trying to keep my wits, but I've arrived. No flailing arms, no screams for help. Just an inert human form.

I'm turning over a woman about my age. She's rather heavy. Later I learn that drowning victims can consume vast quantities of water. I have her on her back now and begin the struggle back to land, one arm across her chest. Some idiot voice in the back of my bedraggled skull bolsters me, shouts, "If you can pull this off you'll be a hero." Every Boy Scout's ultimate dream.

But I've had one quick look at her face. Blue-white skin. Eyes wide open. The water is still five feet deep when I let my feet find the bottom. I curl my toes to get a grip. While she floats on her back, I begin to give her mouth-to-mouth. Precious seconds.

My feet keep moving us shoreward. The impossible, slow weight that I felt while swimming now seems like nothing. She floats, I glide. I keep pumping air into her lungs. Keep trying to ignore what my senses tell me: the empty eyes, the coldness of this desperate kiss. On the rocky shoreline now, a small knot of onlookers has appeared. The spell of the holiday is breaking. Voiceless, lungless, I yell to them for help. I've reached the shallows and her body is on the rocks. It has found the weight of all the sadness in the world. No one moves. A second plea, but still none move. All the old tales are true. No one wants to get this close to tragedy. No one moves to help.

I'm alone on a stumble of kelp and barnacle-laden rocks, kneeling over a woman in a black bathing suit, breathing life back into her. *Trying* to breathe life back into her. The crowd further shoreward suddenly scares me more than anything yet. I feel absolutely and finally alone. Scared out of my wits. My only friend, my only ally, is this woman, this stranger, who so depends on me and me alone for salvation. I've scraped up my legs badly on the sharp rocks. They bleed bright blood. Even as I continue to breathe air into her mouth, I think about how foolish I must look here in my black socks, short pants, and T-shirt. I wonder if they think this is staged. "What is he doing out in the ocean in his socks?" someone might be wondering.

The seconds stretch out, each one longer than the next. It's at times like this I put in an order to God. *Don't do this to me, dammit,* I demand of Him. The tone is wrong, but I can barely think, barely breathe . . . and yet I must continue to administer more air to this helpless woman. *Please,* I repeat to Him. *I'll do anything.*

I am at the bargaining phase of a crisis. It has always worked before. While not a particularly religious person, I've always believed in miracles. And miracles have been performed plentifully in my life. I have reason to expect one now more than ever.

The sky is indifferent; the face before me is lifeless and undemanding. I close my eyes and continue.

Shouts now from the shore. The lifeguards from the other side of the headland have found us. First to arrive is a girl, maybe nineteen, who has run the entire half-mile here. Together we begin to carry the swimmer shoreward, but even with two of us carrying the weight, we're too slow. Better to stay put and work at the resuscitation. She takes over the work as I gulp for air.

A few minutes later, other guards arrive. The first is relieved of breathing. Somebody vomits—maybe the victim, maybe one of the lifeguards. I'm not sure which. Someone begins to pump on the chest.

"Has anyone called an ambulance?" I ask.

No one is sure. With professional people at work here, I decide I should leave and check on the ambulance. I stumble off, over the idiot rocks. Someone in the crowd wants me to stop. He's asking me what happened. I want to curse at him, push him over. Instead, I run past the crowd and begin the ascent up the hill to the tea room, to a phone.

I have not felt such a burning in my chest since I was in high school and ran a mile after having the flu. I pant and heave my way up the embankment. Cresting the hill, I am again in the parking lot. It's like I've entered another world. Tourists linger and look off to sea, kids play with Frisbees. They look at me like I have just arrived from an alien land, a straggling refugee. Inside, I call an ambulance.

Yes, they are on their way. I describe precisely where the woman is. I tell the dispatcher to radio to the ambulance that she is not breathing and her heart has stopped. The dispatcher answers in that classic matter-of-fact way that Nova Scotians sometimes have: "Oh, yeah." As if I had just announced the weather forecast.

I decide I might be able to save some time if I drive down to Stoney Beach and commandeer a four-wheel drive of some sort to travel the rocky rubble to the point and retrieve her, get her closer to the road and ambulance access. I speed off down the hill. There are trucks and Broncos, and a fancy red jeep, but either the drivers aren't around or won't get involved.

Finally, I find a man in his twenties accompanying a blind girl into a truck cab.

"We need you to haul in a person who nearly drowned. Can you drive the shoreline?"

He says yes, then no, then maybe; then he says he has to leave—he has to get his sister home. Damn.

I race back to the top of the hill and wait for the ambulance to arrive. When they get there, I lead the men down the hill. I can see as we descend that she has not moved below, though the lifeguards are still giving CPR. But I begin to admit to myself what I have known all along.

The ambulance men reach her and go to work. Local rescue volunteers are on scene as well. A crowd has gathered around the body now, and I fade back into it, then turn around and leave. I believe that if I don't stay around to hear the pronouncement that somehow a miracle can yet happen. It is a slow, painful drive home. The other beach is still crowded, but it's late in the day, and people are beginning to stream home on the road, back to the city, back to the end of their holiday. It will be off to work in the morning.

At home I tell the story to my wife. I refuse to admit that the woman is dead. Later the RCMP phone, ask me to come file a report. I find out the inevitable. And I also learn the woman's name: Mary Lou. She was thirty-four and the mother of four kids, including a one-year-old. Another person on the scene said Mary-Lou had gone into the water to help a child caught in the same current. The child eventually made it to shore.

> ~ My dear Lesley. "The fact that you tirelessly battled the Nova Scotia government for lifeguards, even when it felt impossible, even if death won, you fought your best fight, twice over. Our mother wasn't the only hero at Stoney Beach on that Canada Day, 1984. It was in your hopeless attempt where you became an angel of Earth."
>
> ~ Jeanine LeBlanc

Wendy grew up in Calgary, Alberta, as the middle child in a family of seven children. With home life fraught with alcoholism and violence, she learned from a very early age how to survive and escape into the worlds of spirit, books, nature, and art. After many traumas, she left Calgary mid-winter to live on the streets of Vancouver when she was sixteen.

Much of the time between then and her first back surgery at twenty was spent hitchhiking and hopping freights as she crossed Canada four times. She also travelled some of the Western coastal States. She deals with chronic pain and the resulting sporadic work times and abilities all while honing her creative process. A great deal of her work has been in the construction and forestry industries to keep her back muscles strong in an effort to avoid ending up in a wheelchair. Now retired, her focus is getting back to her love of photography, sculpting, building, and creating. She also relishes the time she spends with her daughter and grandchildren and hopes to inspire others to reach for the silver linings of life.

Lovingly dedicated to Elissa-Shaye and Brielle, the sparks for my fire within.

# FIRE WITHIN

## *By Wendy L. Clark*

My mother's tears rolled down her cheeks at the news. Most would celebrate, most would rejoice, most would hardly wait to spread the news. Not my mother, not again. She was so sure that the doctor had misdiagnosed her that she quickly set up another appointment with another doctor. Finally, the day came. Nervously, she sat there, wringing the pleats of her skirt, waiting for the receptionist to usher her in.

"These old crones that call themselves doctors don't know shit!" she muttered half aloud, not caring who heard.

She barely heard her name called and slowly got up and reluctantly followed the nurse back. Hating everything about being invaded by the cold gloves, with the stern, judgmental face peering at her from the other side of the sheet, she imagined herself anywhere but there. When that failed to work, she tried to distract herself from reality by counting the stained ceiling tiles. Finally, with the sharp snap of the latex, she braced herself and cringed, waiting for his words to shatter her world. "Mrs. Clark," he finally uttered, "I'm afraid you've got a tumor the size of a football in your uterus—"

She breathed a big sigh of relief and cut him off saying, "I knew that doctor was a quack!" she huffed. Some degree he has, telling me I'm pregnant. "Thank Christ," she continued. "Last thing I need is another mouth to feed."

Stunned, he gently put his hand on hers and stopped her from going on. "I'm going to schedule you for surgery and get that tumor out just as soon as I can, Mrs. Clark. We'll have you up and running after those kids again before you know it!"

*Great,* she thought, *just another damn tumor.*

It wasn't the first nor would it likely be the last, this being the third one she would have removed. Shivers ran through her as she thought of the bullet she had dodged. She couldn't fathom adding to her brood of three and becoming even more entrenched in her marriage with her violent alcoholic husband.

Not much time passed before they had her ready for surgery. She looked forward to the break and succumbed to the anesthetic eagerly. Next thing she knew, she was waking up to that familiar antiseptic stench. As her eyes groggily adjusted to her surroundings, she was shocked to see the doctor's face above hers. Immediately she noticed his look of concern and knew something was amiss.

"Mrs. Clark," he stated, "this may shock you, but you are indeed pregnant."

"But, but . . ." she stammered. "The tumor, you said it was a tumor . . ."

"Yes, we removed the tumor," he said. "It was right there, crowding the baby, and it's a good thing we found it."

He told her to get some rest and that he'd be back the next day. She cried herself to sleep that night, stunned at the news of my coming arrival, and nervous of the journey ahead of her.

A week later, she was allowed to return home, if she took it easy for a while. The stitches were still fresh, red and swollen with pain to match, so it wasn't hard for her to stay on the couch. Suddenly the front door flew open with a thunderous crash. Startled, she twisted painfully to see my father standing in the doorway clutching his familiar thick squared bottle of dark navy rum.

"Oh, you're home, Bitch!" he snarled, and proceeded to tip and guzzle back the mostly full bottle. Upon finishing, he staggered over to her and fell full force with his elbow onto her belly. Upon hearing the commotion and screams, a neighbour managed to get help and an ambulance arrived quickly to take my mother right back to the hospital. My mother described that scene as my delicate, under-developed being needing to be put back into her body and sewn back up. It was confirmed that she was three months' pregnant with me. As fearful as she felt about how she was going to manage with a fourth child, her motherly instincts kicked in and she vowed to protect me and my developing body, not knowing what damage my father had already caused.

My earliest and unclouded memory is of me being around three years old, surrounded by Light Beings, with them conveying to me that this life was going to be extremely difficult. I would need courage, faith, and to remember that I am loved and never alone. These beings came to me in translucent, shimmering colours with all-encompassing forms that enveloped me in a familiar love I understood. Their voices echoed inside my mind while their warmth embraced my new body. I started trying to talk to my mother about reincarnation, knowing that I had just come from somewhere, but she quickly and angrily shut me down. I learned really young to keep those visits and those thoughts to myself.

Fast forward to me as a young woman of sixteen, standing naked in front of a full-length mirror for the first time. I'm looking and seeing a reflection that I'm not familiar with. The only part of the double I recognize is my head, slightly cocked to the right. I knew that well, as I had seen it in every school picture. I also knew all too well that I was skinny and gangly, but I had never visualized that I looked like what I was seeing. My left-hand ribs were compressed and bent in toward my spine, while the right hand ribs were ballooned and double the size of the left and far exceeding the hip. The level of the hips were blatantly off-centre, like a seesaw with just one person. My left leg was an obvious inch and a half longer than the right, and my leaning body reflected that. So, there I stood, mesmerized by this stranger, not really understanding why I hadn't braved a glance before, yet at the same time inwardly knowing the shame my naked body held to the core. She wasn't hurting me, at least physically, so I stuffed her inside my head and told no one for years. Proceeding with my own illusion that nothing was out of the norm, I wasn't going to be affected or concerned about my body being warped. I made it normal in my head by repeating a childhood song about the crooked little man in his crooked little house. All was well in my fantastical imagination.

At twenty years old, I had been working at Western Aluminum—a place that manufactured window frames—for a little over a year. One day I bent forward from the hips to reach the topside of the horizontal window on my workbench. Without a stitch of pain whatsoever, my body locked in at that forty-five-degree angle, making me unable to stand up straight again. I silently tried to deal with it on my own and labored fifteen minutes to no avail.

Helpless and panicked, I called out to my brother-in-law, and he, along with some other co-workers, came to my aid. It had suddenly become clear that the inevitable was here. I would reluctantly expose my crooked frame and get checked out.

My first choice was to go to a chiropractor. After sitting there for a nerve-wracking hour, my name was called. As I stood up, ready and willing to go into my appointment, an ambulance screamed up to the doors. In a flurry of activity, paramedics removed a woman from the back. I walked out.

My next appointment was to an orthopedic surgeon, who informed me that I would either be dead or in a wheelchair for the rest of my life by twenty-five years old if I chose to forego the surgery. He told me not to take too long with my decision as I walked out, stunned by his words. As leery as I was about surgery, I couldn't fight the sting of his foreboding words and decided to go ahead with the operation. Little did I know that I was just one of many guinea pigs for a barbaric and painfully brutal practice to straighten the spine. They screwed and clamped solid steel rods to my newly-sheared spine.

Upon waking from my surgery, the immediate and explosive pain that wracked my body to the core sent my soul careening out of my physical body and into the surrounding dimension where my visitors were, surrounding me with love and reassurance. There they were, assuring me that I indeed could do this, and they would be there supporting me. Embracing me with pure love, they coaxed me to return to my pain-wracked body. In an instant, I was back to endure a nightmare journey that few could imagine.

Aside from the pain of having to learn to walk again and wear a brace fashioned for a straight spine for a year, I also had to endure the poles hitting different nerves alongside my spine. Some days my left arm would swing about, paralyzed, and I would have to use the other to stuff the offending hand in my back pocket until it was useful again.

Other times it would be the right side of my face that was useless, or my right leg would go out and render me crippled. The paralysis kept jumping from limb to limb, body part to body part, coupled with so many different types of pain that it was hard to fathom a future.

One type of pain that is incredibly difficult to endure feels like I'm on fire, deep inside, with no relief. The other types of pain I could manage, but this one has been an unwelcome passenger of my body, mind, and soul for the last forty-five years, daily. With the words "You are never alone" permeating my mind in the toughest moments, I knew my constant companions had not forsaken me, giving me the fortitude to take another step, another breath, in my journey. Sadly, the brutal surgeries failed to straighten my spine or give me any pain-free days.

Years later I watched the exact surgery on TV and cringed at the use of bolt cutters, chisels, and other tools I envisioned coming from some sadist's dungeon. I knew then why my body was wracked with unspeakable pain.

I took up really physical jobs, such as forestry and construction that I thought would keep my back muscles strong and out of a wheelchair. I painfully also managed play baseball as a catcher for several years. I fondly hold these years as some of my most enjoyable times. My work life was sporadic amidst three surgeries and healing, but I persevered. I loved working despite the harsh struggle, and gave it my all when I could. When I could not work, I was either creating and designing within my thoughts or physically with crafts or art when my body could tolerate the movement. These things kept me sane and moving forward.

After five years of excruciating, debilitating pain, the universe blessed me with a daughter whom I carried beyond full term and gave birth to naturally despite her being 9lb., 5oz. Regardless of the poles in my back, pushing for five hours, and busting my tailbone during delivery, this was one of the best, most gratifying days of my life. Looking in my daughter's beautiful, soulful eyes, I knew I wouldn't give up fighting. Someone needed my focus and love to survive.

My journey in pain continues and is a constant companion with varying degrees of hardship, yet my spirit and attitude toward my path has greatly altered. I have managed to self-heal a great amount of my physical ailments that were once so debilitating, while I've taken an attitude of endurance with the stubborn spots. I'm not done eradicating that fire within with my own fire within. My days and nights consist of shifting my focus from creating to design to photography to woodwork to recuperation. I have been blessed with strength, endurance, compassion, and faith that my tomorrows are better than my yesterdays because I insist upon that. My spiritual side acknowledges that I alone hold power on my journey and that it's not what cards I'm dealt, it's how I play the game. I choose my game to be filled with love and light, with little attention to the shards of darkness that desire to envelop me.

I've come to a place of comfort within, knowing that I now hold keys to open the doors of healing others. If enduring this pain serves no other purpose than to inspire just one soul to keep on keeping on, I am more than good with that. There is always a pinpoint of light at the end of our darkened tunnels, even when that light evades us. Although this is just a glimpse into a relatively small portion of my journey, my book of life has many chapters. I will never give up, never give in and never let trauma dim my shine.

I had a mirror to peer within, and in that mirror was my mother—a powerful, strong-willed woman who was shatterproof. Although our struggles were different, the strength that my mother had shown throughout her trials and tribulations surely painted a path showing me just how strong an individual would have to be to carry on. Her fire sparked my fire within, and that's the spark I wish to leave my daughter and granddaughter. May all beings find and nurture their own fire within.

Christine, born in Nova Scotia, Canada, spent two decades living in Hawaii, where she developed a strong interest in spirituality and healing. Her career was sadly cut short by fibromyalgia.

After coming home and witnessing her mother suffer and die with dementia, Christine decided to create a new productive life for herself, serving women like her. She studied and did some self-reflection before deciding to coach and write. She healed herself from fibromyalgia in the process. She started coaching, first women with fibromyalgia; later those whose past trauma and abuse manifested as chronic physical and/or emotional pain, judged to have no medical cure.

Christine created her unique Five-Body self-healing program to teach others to heal themselves from fibromyalgia and other chronic pain conditions by learning to listen to their bodies. Pain is our body crying for attention so we can be healed, not to make us miserable. By doing so, we find out who we are, reclaim the power of our human spirit, and thrive.

Coach, trainer, author, and creator, Christine is a messenger of hope and catalyst to transformation.

# A CHILDHOOD MYSTERY WITH A LIFETIME OF IMPACT

### By Christine Lutely

When I was a little girl, my family lived in a dumpy part of Dartmouth, Nova Scotia, next to the train tracks. I remember homeless people hanging around, Cunard's oil business, and Warner's corner store. I remember living in a shabby house next to other shabby houses on a dirt road. Now, everything is gone except the train tracks.

In 1957, when I was about four, I had the measles. I was put in my parents' room, so my little sister wouldn't get sick. Back then, it was understood that a child with the measles must stay in the dark to prevent blindness. Not trusting the thin curtains, my parents put heavy woollen blankets over each of the two windows.

I survived the measles with my vision intact, but not all was well. It took more than fifty years for me to learn what happened, why I had an out-of-body experience, and how that led me into a repeating cycle of adversity.

My upbringing was authoritarian and Catholic. Rules and fear of authority dominated my young life. Going out after school wasn't allowed. I was to come straight home. I was an A-student throughout school and university.

My high school boyfriend, Ron, and I were inseparable through university, even though we attended different schools. A year after graduating, we married and I felt rescued from the restrictions of my youth. We decided not to have children, and I was glad. I didn't want to raise a child in the way I was raised, in a fog of fear and with stifling rules. Ron and I had a strong friendship, but a weak marriage. I had no idea why sex hurt so much. What I had not comprehended at age four had started playing out as bewildering pain and anxiety. Although Ron was a good man, my marriage to him was doomed before it started.

A decade before Anita Hill made it a mainstream topic, I experienced ongoing sexual harassment and a sexual assault by my boss. Not long after the assault, I had a bad fall and became unable to work because my back injury wouldn't heal. After surgery and several months off work, my boss refused to let me return. I complained to the Human Rights Commission, and the interviewer asked me the right questions to discover the sexual harassment at the bottom of my complaint, and the evidence. My boss was given a golden handshake and fired; I got only $2,000.

My second husband, Len, was abusive. He beat me. Once was enough. I left, but returned after we'd both had counselling. Although he never beat me again, he used psychological abuse to force me to put the proceeds from selling my house into a joint account. He invested and lost it. During my time with Len, I had my first flashbacks.

I was vulnerable and four, lying on my parents' bed with the measles. Lorne, a familiar friend of my parents, was babysitting and in the room with me. I floated to the ceiling, happily playing with a couple huge balloons that had floated up before me, a long wavy white balloon with splashes of pastel colours and a yellow duck. Both balloons touched the ceiling ever so gently. I hovered just below them.

The flashbacks left me unsettled, and I found myself in an emotional state that mimicked my childhood—repressing feelings I couldn't name.

My relationship with Len was short, intense, and often scary. It didn't take long before all I wanted from him was out. I felt excruciating incongruence from experiencing domestic violence and psychological and financial abuse while working as the Executive Director of the Halifax YWCA. I felt it on behalf of women's rights, as a feminist.

During that time, I attended a Bob Procter seminar and enjoyed it so much that I purchased an audio/video program on how to go after my dreams. My dream was to live and work in Hawaii. Under Procter's recorded direction, I visualized my dream with sensory details and emotion, wrote it, read it to myself twice a day, as if it was already true, and acted when inspired. One such action was a vacation to Hawaii to visit the Executive Director of the Honolulu YWCA. Within a year, she offered me a job!

I left Len behind and found myself living and working in paradise. Palm trees, beaches, and beauty were everywhere. I lived in Waikiki, learned hula, and snorkeled with colourful fish and coral. I did work I loved in a beautiful building. I filed for divorce. I was in my glory and feeling as if I'd left all my problems behind. The only wrinkle was my temporary work permit.

Over time, my euphoria dissipated. I didn't continue the practice of visualizing my dreams and believing they had come true, and I was unprepared when things shifted. My wonderful boss decided to retire, and I was asked to apply for the top position. Instead of jumping at the opportunity, I second-guessed myself and my limited understanding of Hawaii's diverse culture. I even wondered if it was too soon for me to know if I wanted to remain in Hawaii. I didn't apply, and the woman who was hired decided to clean house of all management, putting me out of a job and a sponsor for permanent residency.

Because of my skills and experience, I found a new job with a property management company that would sponsor me. Unfortunately, history was about to repeat. In this job, an employee of a client complained to me that her boss had sexually assaulted her. I supported her. It wasn't long before that the same man at this new job had done the same to me. Both ex-Marines, my boss supported her boss. That misogyny and the escalating sexual harassment it caused was more than I could handle; I became anxious and started suffering from intense pain. The fear that had travelled with me since childhood was at an all-time high. I crashed with a breakdown. At forty-four, little did I expect I would be unemployed and remain in pain for twenty years.

The flashbacks returned. In these, I was four and in the bathroom with Lorne. He pulled my panties down and touched me inappropriately. Like all abusers, he bound me to secrecy, telling me that my parents would get mad. I assumed that meant mad at me, and I kept the secret, even from myself.

With a psychiatrist, I explored my past experiences of domestic violence and sexual harassment, as well as the flashbacks. I learned that I had suffered early childhood sexual abuse and formed limiting beliefs about myself and the safety of the world. My life experiences had only reinforced those beliefs. While the work with this doctor helped me to understand my life in general, I was still unable to see and process the specifics of what had happened to me. I was diagnosed with PTSD and major depression. A work friend moved in with me; otherwise, I'd have been hospitalized.

A year later, I was also diagnosed with fibromyalgia, because widespread pain and fatigue had become constant companions. So did Iggy, a little Yorkie gifted by a friend, for companionship.

For years, each week, I spent many hours in physical treatments. A rheumatologist broke up trigger points with needles, did rapid IV infusions of lidocaine to treat the severe pain everywhere (until that was deemed too dangerous), and gave me exercises, ultrasounds, and electrical nerve stimulation. A chiropractor did adjustments, a massage therapist iced and massaged me, and I went to pools for aqua-therapy and swimming in water above eighty-three degrees Fahrenheit, to prevent the after-exercise pain typical of fibro. I saw a pain management specialist for nerve blocks.

Legal appointments fighting for benefits and a settlement added to my stress. My identity vanished. I became a work-disabled fibromyalgia patient. I felt deeply lost and discouraged, constantly on edge.

At a pool session, another fibro patient recommended a spiritual healing center to me. At the center, I replaced strict Catholicism with empowering spirituality and found a new group of friends. I needed a new way of being.

I moved out of town to the northeast shore of Oahu, where rents are less, to a condo on the beach. To keep my newest beloved dog, Bailey, with me, I had her certified as a service animal and, after her death, I trained Pono and had him certified too. We saved and served each other. He still accompanies me everywhere.

In the country, and with little social interaction apart from a small circle of trusted friends, I learned to just be, no longer trying to prove or do things to have value. I leaned into my connection with nature. From the beach, I felt the Hawaiian spirits in the mountains of Punaluu behind me, and the magic of the ocean in front of me. I loved the beauty, and I managed pain by walking, swimming, and doing yoga at the beach.

I met and enjoyed the company of other residents of the condo at our beach, particularly a boy, Michael, who at eleven years old and living with his dad, noticed me because of my dog. Over the years, I sewed on his patches as he worked toward becoming an Eagle Scout. When he honoured me as his Eagle Scout Mom at the ceremony, I was so proud of him and thrilled beyond belief that I'd found a way to support a child in feeling confident and brave.

One day, after my sixtieth birthday, I spent a pleasant afternoon with a casual adult friend, Mick, playing in the waves at our beach. Following our swim, Mick insisted he needed to use my warm shower instead of the unheated pool shower. You might see it coming, but I did not expect to be date raped. I told him, repeatedly, I did not want to have sex. He didn't accept that no means no.

Like my experience at the age of four, I instantly withdrew from the trauma. My focus was on my terror of being beaten again and preventing that. It seemed as if I didn't fully experience the rape, having exited my lower body to manage the situation from inside my head. I bided my time. I didn't feel him pushing into my unwelcoming, unresponsive body, yet I was mentally aware of it happening. As soon as he finished, for some reason, I lightly kissed the top of his head and said, "Get up." Off he went for a shower, suddenly obedient. I redressed and planned how to safely get him out of my apartment.

He came out of the bathroom, and with elevator key in my hand, I led him out of my apartment. I followed an instinct, and as I put him in the elevator, said, "Mick, I think I should know your last name now." I was surprised when he told me. I pushed the button down to the main floor and quickly went to my apartment balcony to watch him leave the property. Once he was out of sight, I took off my favourite bathing suit and tossed it in the garbage, took a long shower, and cried.

I didn't put myself through the ordeal of reporting the rape to the police. I decided to live with the small comfort of knowing it was Mick D. who raped me.

Not long after the rape, I confided in a psychologist and friend who introduced me to EMDR (Eye Movement Desensitization and Reprocessing). After a few associations, she gave me the word 'movie' to associate. Moving my eyes back and forth, I instantly remembered my 1975 flight response, running out of the movie *Tommy* when the kids put a fire hose on the deaf, dumb, and blind kid. I also instantly connected my flight response during that movie to my four-year-old self's dissociation when I was so innocent that I couldn't interpret the horror of what shot on my face. At sixty, I finally became a conscious witness to Lorne's masturbating and ejaculating on my face, after his worse attempts at satisfying himself failed, only because I was too small.

This memory explained my temporomandibular (TMJ) pain, unusually small mouth, and why I grind my teeth at night, not to mention many adverse experiences throughout my life and my numerous escalating health challenges. The original dissociation protected me, but—deeply buried—it created adversity over and over. Finally remembering the secret took away its power.

Now, seven years later, I've come full circle. In 2015, I came back to Nova Scotia to visit my ill mother, and stayed. I started a coaching and training business, working with others who have suffered as I had. After decades away, I was living in a pleasant apartment less than a mile from my childhood home, now long gone, with the area redeveloped as a proper modern entrance to Dartmouth from the Halifax Ferry. I, too, have changed and grown.

At the encouragement of a friend during the winter of 2020, I began to put words to what I've lived and learned. During this time, I accidentally texted Mick D. From our afternoon together and his many unanswered calls to get together again, I had his number in my phone. I'd forgotten it was in there, and through one of those strange series of bumping buttons on the phone in my pocket, a moment of synchronicity happened.

Not recognizing my new phone number, he asked who I was and if I knew him. I replied by text, calling him by his full name and telling him matter-of-factly that after an afternoon playing in the waves together in Hawaii, about seven years before, he ignored my "No" and raped me, in my apartment. He did not deny it.

The universe seemed to know I was now ready to accuse this man. That first offence was so bad that it took nearly fifty-six years to retrieve the dissociated memory that caused so much havoc throughout my life. Ironically, being raped finally instigated the discovery so I could move forward with no secrets from myself, shame-free. Without shame, I share my story in the hope of helping others.

Melonie lives in Nova Scotia, the place she has always wanted to live. Now that she has recovered from daily drug and alcohol addiction, she is exploring her creativity. She is enthusiastic at creating paintings and hopes to one day share them. She is also writing a memoir of life her experiences. Walking her love Sam, an eighteen-year-old dog, brings Melonie some peace and calm. While walking, Melonie calls on the Holy Spirit as she realizes now that finding peace of mind and purpose can take a lifetime.

# PEACE IS A CHOICE

## By Melonie Jackson

For much of my adult life, I drank and did drugs. Eventually, I lost my home, my friends, my faith, and my sanity. It did occur to me that I was out of control, but I wouldn't admit that to anyone . . . not even truly myself. By 2005, I barely had enough self-esteem for anything. So when my younger sister needed help with her kids, I jumped at the chance to move from Toronto to Nova Scotia. I desperately needed to be needed.

By 2008, I got a place to live and a job as a cleaner with Loblaws Superstore. The pay was minimum wage without benefits, but I was grateful to have the job. In May of 2011, I got sober, for almost two months. Then in early July, Loblaws falsely accused me of theft, fired me, and banned me from the store. Angry and frustrated, I drank the day that happened. The next day, I decided that I wasn't going to let Loblaws take my sobriety along with my job.

On July 27th, 2011, two weeks after I'd stopped drinking, when two cops pulled into my driveway, I didn't get scared. I thought they were there about the false accusation. I had the receipt for the item in question, and I was glad for the chance to tell my side of the story. I was also feeling proud of my new sobriety and a sense of hope for my future.

Leading up to this moment, I'd been talking to my mom, June, regularly. When we'd talked during the last several months, mom was happy and supportive. She said she'd travel from Ontario once I had one year sober, and I couldn't wait.

Growing up, both of my parents were alcoholics. Our family life had been tough, with violence on top of the drinking. Now, though, my mom had been sober for thirty-three years. She'd left my dad in 1978 and married Richard in 1985. He was a kind, intelligent, successful man, and my sisters and I liked him. Since life with dad was so rough, I always felt protective toward her. I trusted Richard to be good to her.

Richard had been sober for thirty years, and they were both involved with AA. They were well-respected, attractive, confident, healthy, and well-to-do. As the extrovert, mom attracted people. During her decades of sobriety, she'd sponsored many women.

Over the years, I felt like I'd disappointed mom. She was so strong and sure and always told me, "You can do anything you put your mind to." The problem was, I didn't put my mind to anything, and the drinking and drugs ruled my life. Because of the shame I carried about this, mom and I hadn't had regular contact, but when we did, it was meaningful. Sometimes she'd stay at my place when she came into Toronto for an AA conference. Occasionally, I went to their farm a few hours north of the city to help with the haying.

Now in Nova Scotia, I was sober and serious about it and she was proud of me and so happy. I was becoming the woman that she always believed I could be. Sobriety was like a whole new wonderful world. Although I still had a lot of anxiety, I wasn't sick every morning, I had physical energy, and I was starting to think clearly.

When the cops showed up on July 27th, the officer said, "I think you should sit down for this." Before I had a chance to seat myself, he continued, "Richard and June were found dead in their home yesterday morning."

I didn't know what to say or how to act. My head felt like it was separating from my body, kind of floating, and my breathing was shallow. I felt as though the cops and my partner Norm were waiting for a reaction of some kind. Self-conscious, I immediately buried my fear and confusion. Although my mind was spinning, I didn't cry or scream.

The officer gave me a card and told me to call the detective in charge in Ontario. They suggested I call victim services, which I thought was strange. I saw the compassion in the officer's eyes, and that memory still brings me comfort. I wouldn't be getting too much comfort or compassion from family for the next few years—maybe because my sisters weren't capable of offering it or maybe because I didn't ask.

"I think we need a drink," Norm suggested. "I'll get a bottle of wine."

Surprising myself, I turned to Norm and said, "You go ahead. Not for me." It was like being in the middle of a tragedy and a miracle at the same time. I didn't have an ounce of inner conflict about having a drink. I wasn't even tempted. At that moment, I understood that I had a choice—simple as that. Within the rising panic, a calm inner understanding also awoke in me. I had a choice about drinking. I didn't need to. This revelation was brand new, and even though she was gone, I felt my mom's presence with me.

Later that day, when I talked to the detective in charge, I learned that Richard had shot my mother in the head while she was sleeping. He then shot their dog and pointed the gun to his own abdomen.

The detective instructed me to call J. Miller because he was in charge. Within the next few days, I learned that he was Richard's son in law, as well as the executor of both his father's and my mother's estates. I'd heard about Richard's daughter over the years, but never met her or her husband Jeff.

Jeff had already arranged a double funeral to take place two days later. Even in my confusion, I felt that it shouldn't be a double funeral since Richard had killed my mom. It was a crime, and he was the perpetrator. There was no doubt about that; he left a note. It didn't make sense.

I could tell you about all the messed-up actions and attitudes that made up the aftermath of this crime. I could tell you about how Richard's family from his first marriage—two daughters and their husbands—acted like this was my mom's fault, and therefore her children should be punished and shamed. But rehashing all of that ugliness serves no purpose here. It's enough to say that the police, victim services, and most of the community behaved like no crime had taken place. I think that it was just too hard for them to believe that Richard didn't have a good justification for what he'd done. After all, he was such a nice man. After three years of brutal negotiations, without empathy, consideration, or fairness toward me and my sisters, Richard's family from his first marriage inherited all of their dad's estate and more than half of my mom's.

I had nightmares for a long time. Eventually, I wondered how people could continue on carrying so much pain and suffering. As I questioned my self-worth and everything I did and didn't do following mom's death, my only comfort was that I wasn't drinking anymore. To help me with the panic attacks I was having, my family doctor prescribed Lorazepam. Of course, I quickly became dependent on it. Given my addiction history, I knew it wasn't good for me, but the doctors kept saying, "It's a low dose. You have anxiety. Keep taking it."

Five years later, even though I wasn't tapering the dose, I was going through withdrawal. I had to either increase it or stop taking it, so I chose to stop. It was one of the most trying times in my life. It took more than a year of strange and awful sensations and panic attacks, but I got free of it.

That same Fall, although I'd never been before in my life, I started going to church. A friend of a friend picked me up every Sunday morning on the way. I prayed and, once, I even cried while standing in line waiting to feel the presence of the Holy Spirit. The church people told me to forgive, but they didn't tell me how. I felt that they weren't all that sincere.

I went to different churches looking for help, and I read a lot of books. Emmet Fox's The Sermon on the Mount: The Key to Success in Life was the one that stuck and felt especially relevant to me as a recovering alcoholic. I began to feel a familiar presence and a comfort, inside of myself, and I recognized this as the same one I'd felt during my worst drug overdose. Back then, I thought of this presence as angels, but unconnected to any organized religion. Now I know that this presence, what I call spirit, is something that's been in and with me at all times, including when I found out my mom had been killed. Now I call on spirit daily, and it feels like comfort, safety, calm.

In retrospect, I think that the cover up of Richard's murder of my mom was influenced by the fact that Russell Williams' crimes were about to hit the news. He and Richard were both Air Force pilots, had lived and/or worked in Ontario, and murdered women. Williams was convicted and jailed in the fall of 2011. One morning during the Williams' investigation, Richard shot my mom in the head while she was still asleep. Was the Air Force too embarrassed by all of this to allow for another conviction? I wonder how a man can shoot his wife in the head while she's sleeping and be praised at a funeral days later. The fact that his son in law was in charge and the police didn't see a conflict of interest, helped serve to keep it silent.

Richard left a note saying, "I can't live the lie anymore." I'll never know his reasoning, but I've found within myself some empathy for him. Whatever he was thinking or feeling must have been extreme.

I read somewhere that in Canada, one woman is murdered by her spouse every week. We need to be aware of this and say it's not okay. At the funeral, I wish I'd stood up and said, "This is all wrong." Since mom was murdered, I've felt burdened by the sense that I must represent her properly, get some justice and truth, and make up for what I didn't do at the time. I've felt great sadness that my sisters and I haven't been able to come together in all of this. Maybe one day we will. Who knows what the future holds?

I struggle to accept that so many men feel justified to take a life and that society seems to accept it. Denial and deceit have dominated mom's death and the aftermath of it, all of which delayed healing and closure. There was no good reason for what Richard Brown did; it was not a 'righteous act' as it has been represented. I hope that in telling the truth, as far as I know it, some good will come.

Nine years later, I'm realizing, a bit at a time, one revelation after another, that all I need to do is accept the things I can't change, choose to be free, and live. Throughout these years of learning how to think, feel and accept all of what's happened, my biggest revelation has been that all is well if I let it be.

Slowly, I've been remembering who I am. Early in my life, mom used to encourage me to paint with water colors and acrylics. Now I've found my way back to painting, and it turns out I really do have talent. I started working with horses, and it was healing to be around them. I also had the feeling I should return to the job I'd been fired from. It took courage, but I followed my inner guidance that it didn't matter if they rejected me. What mattered was that I try. It turned out the person who falsely accused me had left, and I was able to go back to work.

Several years ago, mom came to say goodbye to me in a dream. She was standing with Richard and smiling, and she said, "I'm leaving now." I knew she wasn't worried about me and that she didn't want me to be anyone other than who I was. All the expectations that I thought she had for me were just coming from me in the first place, from my imagination and self-recrimination. She used to say, "You can do anything that you put your mind to" and I now realize that's all she meant. That's all I needed to know.

In those months before her death, I heard her joy and the love of life in her voice. The way mom died does not take away from the way she lived. While she lived, she got free and was happy and healthy. The way for me to honour her is to free myself from my imagined chains and to respect myself. My plans are to stay sober, let go of the past, and continue forward in a healthy direction.

I'm not interested in convincing others to agree with me or in proving a point. I'm no longer trying to prove that I'm worthy, or that my mom didn't deserve to die like she did. In my heart, I already know that all of that is true. I understand that peace is a choice, so I choose it.

Mark Kennedy grew up in a loving family with his parents, Gary and Paula, and older sister, Tracey Andrews. He was born and raised in Cape Breton in a small community called Westmount. He graduated from Riverview Rural High School in 1995 and continued his education at UCCB (University College of Cape Breton), which is now called CBU. Mark completed his bachelor's degree in electrical engineering at Dalhousie University in 2002. Currently Mark lives and works in Halifax, Nova Scotia. He is a very proud father of two amazing girls, Riley and Emiley Kennedy. In his spare time, Mark enjoys running, going to the gym, hiking, walking, and biking. Last but certainly not least, he loves spending quality time with family and friends.

# BECOMING THE NEW ME

## *Mark Kennedy*

O n the evening of December 16th, 2016, my wife and I were watching TV. It was chilly out, but our pellet stove kept the basement cozy and warm. As she napped on the lazy boy, I went upstairs to the kitchen to get a snack. When I saw her cell phone resting on the half wall that divided our kitchen and the stairs to the basement, I had a gut feeling that I should take a look at it. I wasn't sure what to do. For most of my life, I hadn't known what to do with my feelings, other than push them down and out of sight.

For the past seven or eight months, my wife and I had been having some marital problems. I knew we both needed to work on things in order to get back on track. Although I'd never done something like it before that night, the nagging feeling wouldn't let go and I picked up her phone. As I looked through the text messages, the worst thing I could imagine happened. One text in particular, sent to the girlfriend she was supposed to have been out with the night before, made my worst fears into harsh reality.

My stomach dropped and turned into knots, my heart raced out of control, and my face got hot. In shock at what I'd just read, I was shaking. The text message revealed that my wife was having an affair. I couldn't believe this was happening to me and our family. We had two beautiful daughters, seven and nine years old. We had a lovely family home, fully paid off, and we both had good paying jobs we enjoyed. Between dating and our marriage, we'd been together for twenty years. Knowing that my wife, who I loved and trusted, had been living a second life behind my back hurt beyond words.

Almost immediately after reading the text, I called the two people I trust the most, the people who are also my best friends: my parents, who were also shocked. A four-and-a-half hour drive away from me in Cape Breton, it was one of those times I wished the distance between us was seconds instead of hours. I needed them to listen and to help me figure out what to do, and they suggested I talk to my wife.

When I went downstairs and woke up my wife, I asked her straight up if she was having an affair. She cried and said yes, telling me the identity of the other person. I knew him—someone I considered a friend. Many years before, we'd met working together and eventually became friends. Our families would even get together at their cottage in the summertime. My wife and I and our kids, along with his wife and son. It felt like someone had stabbed me in the heart. The whole situation was devastating.

From there, things got progressively worse for me. I wasn't sleeping; I was depressed. As I couldn't function in my current role as a project manager, I left my job in February. In April, I did eventually find a new job, a sales role still supporting the construction industry in which I've always worked. My wife and I tried to work on things and went to couples counselling, but it wasn't helping. In August of 2017, we finally decided we needed to separate. I was heartbroken and totally lost. I had no idea how to deal with the overwhelming sadness I felt.

One evening in October, my wife and I were at the house packing things up and getting things ready to sell. She was going to be moving into one of our rental properties, and I was going to stay in the house until it sold. That night we had an argument over our separation agreement, particularly the spousal and maintenance support payments. I became very upset and needed an outlet for my anger.

Honestly, even before I found out my wife was having an affair, I'd often wake up angry and unsure what to do about our relationship. Ten years of military training on top of cultural conditioning had bred into me the lesson that men weren't supposed to show or discuss emotions, but that hadn't stopped me from feeling them. Leaders were supposed to be strong. Men were supposed to be strong. The only thing I knew to do to release all of the built-up tension I felt was to physically express it—sometimes this meant sports or exercise, and sometimes this meant punching a hole into the wall. That night it meant I took a plastic bottle of orange juice from the fridge and threw it against the road outside. Still upset and full of frustration, I left to go play hockey.

When I got back home, my wife, two girls and my mother-in-law were just about packed up and leaving. I asked what in the world was going on. "That's it," my wife said. "We are done. I'm leaving and taking the girls with me right now." I wanted to talk with her, but when I tried, her mom got right in front of me and insisted that they were leaving, telling me how foolish it was to get so upset about the money. I could hear my girls crying in their rooms.

At this point, I knew I was losing everything. My wife was leaving and taking the kids. That realization coupled with the anger consumed me. Before I knew it, I grabbed a knife from the kitchen and left the house. I jumped into the car and drove for about five minutes to a dead-end street where I usually went for walks with the dog. When I went into the woods that night, my full intention was not to come out. I was going to end my own life. Blinded by rage, I thought the separation agreement would completely destroy my income and I would be broke. My wife and daughters would all be gone from my life. What else was there left to live for?

From in the woods, I heard other cars and then talking. I realized my wife had called the police. I could hear them looking for me with their tracking dog, and I could see their flashlights in the distance. For many hours that night, I hid. I sat under a tree, not moving an inch. The night was crisp, and although I had a jacket on, I was still cold. The moon was out, and I could smell the spruce needles. Other than the sounds of the police looking for me, the woods were silent.

From my vantage point under the spruce tree, I could glimpse the police cars and an ambulance parked by my car. If I looked up at a forty-five degree angle, I had a clear view of the sky. I forced myself to think of a happy time. The first thing that came to mind was my own wedding. I'd always absolutely loved weddings, and my own had been my favourite of them all. Then my mind put me into two specific events in the future: the wedding days of my two daughters. I imagined what it would be like to only be able to look down at these precious moments from the skies and clouds above. I imagined what it would be like for my girls and how they would need their daddy with and beside them, holding their arms as I walked them up that aisle. But I wasn't there. It felt so real. How could I be so selfish and ruin what should be the happiest day of their lives? I didn't ever want to do that to them.

Ultimately, for the sake of my daughters, I decided to come out of the woods that night and fight to live on. I walked out of the woods and onto the road by myself. No one had to force me. The police were waiting for me, and the ambulance took me to the hospital. At the hospital, I waited for hours and hours. When the doctor finally saw me, he said, and I quote, "Things get tough. You just have to deal with it." He then asked me if I was going to do this again.

"No," I said, "of course not."

I was released right away. No questions or follow-ups at all. Overwhelmed with emotion and loss, I had almost ended my own life that night, and all in all, the doctor spent five minutes with me. I felt so sad, not just for myself, but for everyone else who'd experienced this kind of treatment.

Because of my actions that night, I lost custody of my girls. I knew I was heading down the wrong road. This was the turning point in my healing when I decided to become the new me. I had to get my girls back in my life. I knew it would take time and hard work, but I needed to recover and fix things in myself. I didn't want to be someone who lost their temper and threw things or punched things and put holes in the walls. I did not want my kids to be scared of me. I didn't want to be someone who woke up in the morning pissed off and not understanding why. I began to understand how my behaviour was part of my wife leaving me. These feelings and actions had to change. I wanted to get my girls back and be an amazing dad, I wanted to lose the anger issues I had, and I wanted to be an overall better person.

Through the Nova Scotia Health Authority, I was fortunate enough to get a referral. I saw a mental health counsellor which helped tremendously. Because the referral came from my doctor, treatment was completely covered by the system. I also read a ton of books, and had tremendous support from so many people: my parents, sister, uncle, aunts, cousins, work colleagues, and close friends, as well as my brother-in-law and mother-in-law.

They listened to me repeatedly. They cried with me, asked me questions, and were so genuine. They made sure to include me in their outings, and call and text me. It was incredible, and I am beyond grateful. There's no way I could have made it this far without all of them in my life.

For two years, I worked hard to unlearn what I'd been taught about being a man. I came to understand that in real life and everyday relationships, not showing emotion was the worst thing I could do. Being able to talk and communicate my inner feelings is vital. I found that I just needed someone I could trust and with whom I could simply talk about how I felt. For me, this started in therapy, which was a huge part of how I lost that inner anger, stopped waking up pissed off every morning, and learned healthy ways to deal with tough emotions. Now, when something is bothering me, I talk about it and I feel better.

I also had to take a close look at my job. Previously, I'd worked many long hours and travelled, being away from home way too much. This caused me a great deal of stress. Sure, it's great to have lots of money, but in the grand scheme of things, it doesn't mean too much. It meant much more to me to be able to spend time with my daughters, family, and friends in a relaxed way.

I wish I could have learned all of this sooner in my life. I am truly sorry for all that I did and didn't do that led to the end of my marriage. The person I am now versus the older version of myself is like night and day. I'm not sure I would have changed much if this situation hadn't happened to me. All I can say is that this life-altering situation became something new and powerful. I had to continue to grow and learn, to get better, and to move forward. This is why I've also forgiven the people who hurt me. In the end, I'm better for all of it.

So let's fast forward to present day, May of 2020. For two years, I've had my girls back with me, now fifty percent of the time. In September of 2019, I was able to buy myself another house. My ex-wife and I have an amicable relationship, and I'm very proud of that. I've dealt with my long-time internal anger issues, and most importantly, I can talk about my true feelings and emotions. I communicate and express them freely. I have a wonderful, more powerful and connected relationship with my daughters than ever before.

Just recently, I was watching a movie with them, and they noticed I was crying. They asked, "Are you okay?" In the past when I'd watch movies with my family, during sad points I made sure never to cry. As I'd done for most of my life, I would push those feelings away. Now when I see something sad or moving, I no longer hide it. I cry to let it out. This time when the girls asked if I was okay, I smiled at them and said, "Yes absolutely. It's healthy to cry when you feel sad." It felt like a big moment for all of us.

This relationship with my girls is my personal reality check that I've become someone I like. I'm happy with myself now, and that's major in my book.

Anne was born in the 1950s and grew up in a family besieged with allopathic medicine. For twenty years she studied the human body and how to heal alternatively, as both of her parents and her sister passed away from prescription medicines. This began her lifelong journey to (re-)learn all she could to heal at the source. Over the years, Anne learned to live openly and confidently as a lesbian, teacher, and healer, authentically and with integrity. She now channels and teaches over thirty energetic ancient healing arts.

As an author, writing has always been a passion for her. She has also enjoyed farming, working as a landscape foreman, and cultivating. In 2019, Anne moved to the central Okanagan in British Columbia; a journey toward the change she longed for.

# TIME TO HEAL MYSELF

## *By Anne Clarke*

I'm a healer. But I wasn't always a healer. About twenty years ago, I learned Reiki. Since, I've processed significant childhood trauma and healed from ailments that took a page and a half to list. I went from twenty-two pills a day and two hearing aids to zero. I figured I was invincible . . . until March 2019.

I was in Calgary, walking my dog Aurora, a two-year-old shepherd-collie cross. On our return trip home, I saw a little red sports car drive by, turn around, and park in front of my house. I thought nothing of it, as there were people standing on the road across from this fellow's car and he seemed to be talking to them.

Aurora and I crossed the street at the corner, followed the sidewalk past his vehicle, then walked up the steps to the house. I unlocked the door, entered, and proceeded to remove Aurora's leash with my back to the door.

Unbeknownst to me, the fellow with the sports car had exited his vehicle and followed us up the steps. Up until that point, I'd never had reason to lock the screen door.

At first, though he walked into my residence uninvited, this man seemed calm and rational. He appeared to be in his late forties or early fifties and stood at least 5'10". He was heavy set, well over 200 lbs. At 60 years old, I stood 5'5" and weighed about 170 lbs. Oddly, he was wearing pyjamas. He revealed his name and disclosed that he was a gay, married man, living around the corner from me. He stepped in so close that I smelled alcohol on his breath. That was about the time that his demeanor changed. My body began to vibrate as I sensed how vulnerable I was in that moment.

He said that I knew him. He said that I telepathically called him to me. I'd never met him, and I felt like he was trying to convince me of familiarity in a brainwashing kind of way. Although my body was shaking, I was frozen in extreme shock.

I watched him pass by and walk into the kitchen. He asked me what I'd eaten for breakfast and opened the fridge door. He drew a carton of eggs from the fridge and placed two in a pot of water. I was baffled. I had no idea what was going to happen next. Time seemed to stand still while the eggs cooked. Once boiled, he placed the eggs on a plate on the counter.

He asked me if there was anyone else in the house. I said, "Yes, two men downstairs."

He asked if he could use the washroom. I said yes.

The only door that was open was the bathroom door at the end of the hall. He opened the other closed doors one at a time. I asked him to be respectful and just go to the bathroom.

I broke through the shock and used the time to text the men that rented one of the suites downstairs for help. They responded that they'd called 9-1-1 and the police would be there in five to ten minutes. As I couldn't move, I hoped it was true. When the man returned, he asked me to hold and squeeze him as tightly as I could. My thoughts raced. Is he trying to see how strong I am? I refused. Then he asked me to hit him as hard as I could in the face. I refused. He asked me if he could hit me in the face as hard as he could. I refused again. Now I felt my inner self vibrating along with my body. Fear gripped me.

Suddenly, he said that he and I were going to Banff. He grabbed me from the front and tried to drag me from the kitchen in the back of the house toward the front door. My big toes were the only parts of me touching the ground. He squeezed me so tightly that pain ripped through my left shoulder. I escaped his grip, and though I was almost paralyzed with fear, I kept calmly talking to him, trying to ignore the shooting pain and keep calm myself. I felt like I was going to die somewhere. In the house? In Banff? The trembling in my whole body increased.

He moved to the back hall and yelled downstairs. When one of the men downstairs yelled back, his face got red and he began shouting and slamming the door, over and over. He eventually went down onto the first landing to engage with the men downstairs, and at that point I slammed the upstairs door and locked it, running to the front door to deadbolt it as well.

I had a torn rotator cuff and was left to suffer with PTSD. My perpetrator was only charged with mischief for attempting to shatter the front window of the house after I'd locked him out. The police said they were unable to charge him with anything more.

While all of this transpired, the woman I was in a relationship with at the time had been at work. When she got home, she was less concerned about me than her Buddha statue the man had broken to hit the front window. I wondered why she didn't love me enough to care about what had happened to me. Was I not worthy of that kind of love?

For me, the incident was an awakening. It brought up fifty-six-year-old issues that I thought I'd already dealt with. I hadn't.

Because I was suffering from PTSD from the assault, I called Victim Services and was awarded five therapy sessions. During those sessions, I learned that I was in an emotionally abusive relationship with the woman I was living with. Learning this was part of an even bigger realization.

Later, sitting in my living room in Calgary, not far from where the man had broken into my home and assaulted me, I travelled back in time to when I was four years old, having just started kindergarten. I recalled my classmates going on a weekend field trip to a farm. My parents had other plans and drove me to the dairy farm where my sister lived. The first fateful night of that weekend, I remembered I was wearing a soft flannel nighty, and I remembered waking up to what I now know was sexual molestation. Back then, I just knew that I was being touched in a place that felt very uncomfortable at best and extremely frightening at worst. The man who sexually assaulted me was someone who had married into the family. He even admitted it in the 90s. My sister's reaction when I told her shortly after was, "don't tell the family or they won't let him come to family functions." I needed my sister to love me. There was not even the offer of a hug. Nothing. I was so scared that, to this day, I wonder why my mind didn't split.

Once back at school after that weekend, I heard about a classmate falling into a bull pen while on the field trip. At that moment, I would've given anything to be that child.

For six long years, I was sexually assaulted by the same man. Following those years, my parents invited two of my cousins to live in our home. During their stay, one of my cousins raped me. What struck me as odd, thinking back, was that he told me that the person who had sexually assaulted me for all those years told him it was okay to rape me.

All this looking back had made me realize that I had become a serial victim. There in my living room, overthinking to the point of exhaustion and tears, after all those years of so many modalities of therapy, I felt it had all been for naught. My childhood had been taken from me, and here I was decades later still suffering in similar ways, not only from the physical assaults but also my current relationship.

My therapist said it would be in my best interest to begin a new journey, and I agreed. It was time to change and act like I was worth something good. It was time to take my power back.

I knew I wanted to leave my city life and head out on my own, but I struggled with this idea after the home invasion. Also, although I'd lived on farms in the past and craved that life again, memories of that first sexual assault lingered. Some nights I still woke screaming at what surfaced in my dreams.

Early one morning, just over two months later, I heard a loud noise coming from the roadway in front of our house. Whoever had done it was gone, but I found the steering column of my Jeep torn apart and the ignition switch destroyed. My Jeep would not allow them to steal it, but I was left with a beautiful shell of a vehicle whose insides would not run. Was this another push toward country living? As the tow truck carried my Jeep away, I finally decided to head West. I ended my relationship and got rid of most of my possessions. In the end, each thing that I purged made me feel better and lighter.

I left on July 4th, Independence Day in the United States. How apropos. At that moment, I realized that, deep in my heart, independence had been one of my goals for a long while. Our journey (Aurora's and mine) had begun.

I drove my son's truck, towing an old seventeen-foot trailer from the 1970s. On our way, Aurora and I stopped at two campgrounds. At the first, my friend Wanda came to visit. She helped me set up my gazebo and also took some of the things I was purging too. My friend Melisa and her mom Dawn met me at the next campground in Carstairs. After supper at the picnic table, we enjoyed a cool lemonade together at the campfire. On my move toward independence, I felt supported.

After visiting campgrounds and good friends' places, we left Alberta and drove West. By the middle of August, Aurora and I ended up in Vernon, B.C. In getting settled, I met new and old friends who showed me around so I could familiarize myself with the area and find a job.

For a while, I'd felt that I needed to do some physical work—I find it good for the soul. So, the first place I applied was at a farm. I got hired and started the next day, assisting an elderly couple with their fruit stand and occasionally picking fruits and vegetables. They'd been there selling their wares for forty-five years and really needed my help. I felt like God had sent me to them and I was very grateful.

At this point, I realized that I am always at the place I need to be when I am supposed to be there. Call it God's divine plan or synchronicity, but don't call it coincidence. That I don't believe in. I worked for minimum wage, nine to ten hours a day, seven days a week, and it felt good. Forty-five years earlier, when I was fifteen, my first job had been picking green and wax beans on a farm for fifty cents a bushel. I'd come full circle.

During that time, I came across the work of world-renowned therapist Marisa Peer. She works with a number of celebrities and speaks often of the high number of suicides among that community. What all those people had in common was the sense that they were not worthy, not enough. I could relate, deeply.

At the beginning of October, the season and my stint at the farm ended. I had already begun a new relationship with a woman, and autumn felt like a great time to move in together. At first, I was glad to be close with someone again and to look for another job—maybe healing work, maybe something else. Since several of my Rubbermaid bins with significant forms had been damaged during my move, I had to throw the contents out. Papers such as receipts, bank statements, and T4 slips that I had saved for several years for my taxes were destroyed by mould, rain, and hail. I walked ninety kilometres in November to acquire what I needed in order to get financial help. Then I was forced to jump through several government hoops to get what I needed to apply for work. I was exhausted.

Then came weeks of what seemed like spiritual, mental, emotional, and physical torture. Many dark nights of the soul. Memories flooding back. Doubting the value of my life. My new relationship echoed old patterns of abuse and became another thing I needed to heal from. For weeks, I felt sick with what I now believe was formaldehyde poisoning. The person I lived with didn't realize ventilation is a necessity in a motor home. I had a window open and, without my knowledge, she closed it. There were three caution warnings in the back closet saying to *always* have ventilation. There is formaldehyde in the wood used to make trailers and motor homes. It gets toxic with no ventilation. I had all the symptoms.

During this time, listening to Marisa Peer on YouTube was one of the things that kept me going, reminding me that I was worthy of life. It's funny how this woman changed my life without ever meeting me. I gave myself Reiki treatments daily and started writing stories of my experiences. Some pretty dark memories spilled out, but many good ones did too. The writing lightened the burdens on my soul.

Due to both PTSD and the shoulder injuries that turned out to be much more than a torn rotator cuff, I had to stop looking for work and get on Persons With Disabilities (PWD). Instead of finding a job as a healer, I finally realized I needed to focus on healing myself.

In the new year, I left my unhealthy relationship and moved in with a new platonic roommate. Since he has two dogs and a cat, Aurora has new friends too. We all get along well, and I now have the energy and healthy space I need to finish the two books that I'm writing: *The Amazing Journey of a Cheese Omelette* and *The Healer, an Autobiography*. I've also met and begun dating a wonderful woman, and I'm the happiest I've ever been. She is my twin flame; this I know for sure. We are independent, yet one.

I've learned that I'm the only person who can hold me back. No one other than myself can keep me from my destiny and purpose. Most of all, I've learned that I am worthy, and I am enough.

This summer, I'm going back to work part-time at the fruit and veggie stand, which is also part of my healing—a chance to reconnect with farm life and make new positive memories. Having come full circle, I now have the opportunity to make the next trip around a better one.

Alberta born and raised, Pamela Dow-Leeks is a proud mother of four children, a newlywed, and an animal lover. She has put fourteen years on the roller derby track, where she is known as "Cakes," and works to cultivate the sport in her community and around the world. She believes in human connection and that we need to feel loved, valued, and supported to be happy and healthy.

Pamela has had to overcome many struggles in life to get to where she is today. She has lost many loved ones to addiction and mental health issues, which led her to follow her passion of working with the most vulnerable in her community.

Pamela has helped host events to stop the stigma associated with the struggles of mental health and honour those who have lost their battle. She hopes to keep spreading awareness to let people know they are not alone.

# FOREVER HER VOICE

## By Pamela Dow-Leeks

On the day before my 34th birthday, I got the call that would forever change my life. "I don't see her," my friend Samantha said. Her being Erin, our mutual friend and my best friend. In my gut, I knew something was wrong. My heart sank and my mind spun out of control. As soon as I finished work for the day, I was planning to head to Erin's to check on her. I hadn't heard from her in several days, which was unusual for us. Our last conversation had consisted of Erin asking me if I wanted her to make me a birthday cake and planning our float down the Red Deer River to celebrate. I knew Erin was stressed, so I told her not to worry about the cake.

Looking back now, I wish I'd been needy. I wish I'd let her know her value, how much her talents were appreciated, and just how damn much I loved her. However, in my attempt not to add things to her plate, I was nonchalant. You know, the kind of conversation when things need to be said, but you don't because you believe you have time and will get to it later.

Erin and I had the type of friendship most people envy. She was my every day, and as I was told at her service by a kind relative, I was one of her soulmates. Erin and I were both single parents and supported each other in our trials and tribulations. We had a way of being each other's voice. Beyond that, we had a mutual love for the sport of roller derby. We travelled to practices and to countless events as volunteers together. For four years, we worked hard to excel and make a name for ourselves, practicing multiple times a week and playing many weekends. We'd joke about being the perfect ten, an amazing jammer-blocker pair and quite the package deal for any team that asked us to play.

Erin was so kind and generous, and her energy was infectious. The first one to start the wave in getting the crowd pumped up at any given event, she was always laughing, smiling, and offering hugs. She always made sure her teammates' gear, even the smelly skates and jerseys, was in top notch shape. She was selfless in her attempts to include others and serve those who mattered to her. When we were around her, we all couldn't help but smile.

Roller derby is a physical sport, full contact on cement floors. Our bodies have taken more of a beating then most adults would ever imagine inflicting on themselves. It was, however, our release and escape, our time away from the stresses of daily life. During our friendship—and most certainly before we'd met—Erin took on more than her fair share. She was the mother of an autistic child, running her own home business, and struggling with a difficult divorce.

Prior to that life-changing phone call, I knew my friend was having a hard time—mentally, emotionally, and physically. Erin had sustained a pretty serious knee injury and since her identity was so wrapped up in roller derby, not being able to play hit her hard. Unfortunately, I was in an ongoing battle over my four kids with their father and working to recover from a mentally abusive and toxic relationship. Looking back, I still wonder if I might not have been as emotionally available as I would have liked or as Erin needed.

Although I encouraged Erin to take time to heal her injury, I didn't talk with her about how she felt about it. As someone whose love language is acts of service, I tried to be there to help her with her projects and give her a break from the everyday stress. I gave her what felt like support to me, but I don't think that's what Erin really needed.

I knew she was on various medications for Lupus and pain from other injuries, but I now know she was also on an antidepressant in an attempt to improve her mental health. I was helping by keeping Erin's life going on the surface while she was doing the best she could to cope with the turmoil underneath. Because I didn't want to make it worse, I didn't acknowledge her emotional pain. I kept our interactions busy with practical things like cutting fabric for her business, making dinner for her kids, or cleaning the house.

On that life changing day, I suggested to our mutual friend Samantha that she check for Erin in the back shed with the hot tub. I felt an overwhelming sense of panic, but pushed it down. In hindsight, I should have just gone to Erin's house myself as originally planned. Instead, still consumed with work and a false sense of hope, I hung up the phone. I awaited a call back letting me know that everything was fine. Unfortunately, the call confirmed the worst possible outcome. My best friend was no longer alive. I felt helpless and broken, overcome with the finality of the situation.

I felt so sorry for Samantha and the heartbreaking sadness and helplessness in her voice. For the trauma of finding someone she loved in such a way and being unable to change anything.

That day, Erin's sons lost their mother, her parents lost a daughter, her siblings lost their sister, the United Way lost an advocate, our teammates lost their jammer and friend, and I lost my 'every day.'

I sprang into motion, trying to arrange the most suitable way to honour Erin's life. I moved from project to project, person, place, and thing. I moved, never stopping to fully process what I'd lost, focusing instead on the many people looking to me for answers as to how we could honour Erin's life and cope with this loss. It seemed to me that my good intentions were met by some people with misunderstanding. I felt like I couldn't do anything right. I was told to be quiet or that I was disrespecting my friend's memory by being honest about her mental health struggles.

During this time, I knew I had one job, and that was to mourn the loss of my best friend. Instead, I ran myself ragged, staying as busy as I could. I helped plan two services, one for the family and one for the roller derby community. I helped with the kids when needed. Through it all, I avoided feeling that empty place inside and dealing with the guilt that was consuming me. Nobody would ever be as upset with me as I was for not knowing what Erin needed. I was lost.

Once things settled, as they always do after life-changing moments, the world went quiet. I couldn't bear it, so I packed up my family for a fresh start. In an attempt to make things easier for my kids, we moved closer to their father. I couldn't imagine that having a grief-stricken mother was much fun, and I knew they were suffering their own loss of Erin, the derby momma they'd grown to love and look up to. Also, I needed to be in a place where nobody looked at me with pity or disdain when I walked into the room. New people, new places, but the same coping mechanisms for me.

I jumped into work—three jobs, four kids, and a new life. I didn't want to feel the loss, so I worked. I kept moving forward. I did have support from home and the amazing people who have always been incredible cheerleaders for me. These friends and family loved me, knowing I was doing the best I could with the hand I was dealt, and always telling me, "You got this." On some level, I also knew I was doing the best I could.

Still, I had lessons I needed to learn and a whole string of heartbreaks I never saw coming. In the two years after Erin's death, I'd lost five more loved ones to tragic accidents and mental health struggles. My poor broken heart had no time to pause and recover, but somehow I found new inner strength and used it to relate to those who needed me and helped them navigate the losses we all now faced. Although I gained new experiences and made friends I will love and cherish forever, after three years away, it was time to go home to be closer to the family and friends I'd left behind. So much more was waiting for me.

From the immediate shock of Erin's death and the loss of other loved ones, I could see what I could or should have done differently. The best way to honour a lesson is to learn from it, so I've taken the time to educate myself and others about the importance of being honest about mental health and not being reluctant to ask for help. I'm loudly working to remove the stigma, and I now know to ask those around me what they need from me so I can support them how they need to be supported, whenever possible.

I realize I may have encountered some backlash from people who were also coping the best way they knew how, as well as those suffering from the stigma surrounding mental health. I've learned not to take it personally. I know there are times I'll provoke a reaction in others. To be able to bring about change, I know I need to speak up, be honest, and show people they're not alone so they can also speak up about their mental health struggles in turn. This isn't easy, but it is necessary. I'm so thankful to all who work alongside me in these efforts.

I also realize I was surrounded by incredible love and support. I had friends drop everything to help me move through the preparations to memorialize Erin's death, and to create an annual Stitch-Rip-Her Memorial Event to honour her. In Erin's name, we've hosted multiple events to raise awareness about mental health issues and sponsored families going through this same struggle and loss. I've evolved out of my guilt and into a person who holds my head high when I walk into the room. I've come to terms with my own flaws and the reactions of others. Although I still like to keep busy and am usually helping or taking care of those closest to me, I'm working to find a better balance. It's important for me to make time to check in with my own self-care and to say no when I need to.

As I became more accepting of myself, I worked hard to set boundaries and believe I was worthy of being loved. In following my heart, I now live in the same town as Erin used to. This place holds so many memories, and I'm surrounded by so much love and beauty. I met the most amazing and patient man, who reminds me to slow down and isn't afraid to dance with me in the kitchen. He never makes me feel bad about how I cope and supports whatever project I'm brave enough to take on.

I knew he was the one for me when, on our very first date, he listened. He listened as I shared years of heartbreak, loss and struggle, and he accepted me anyways. I have no doubt my best friend helped me find my way to this man. He has the same kind of generous heart and gentleness that Erin had. As with her, when people meet him, they can't help but be drawn to his peaceful, positive energy.

We got married on my fortieth birthday, which was also the sixth anniversary of Erin's passing. I started and stopped writing this essay, doubting my ability to say what needs to be said and not wanting to inflict any pain on anyone who misses Erin the way I do. With little nudges from the universe, I pressed on. Our story needed to be told.

At my wedding, we gathered with friends who were there for me at Erin's funeral and the new friends I've made along the way. We filled the day with so much love and laughter. Weeks of rain continued on the wedding day—not the weather a bride would've hoped for an outdoor summer ceremony. But with angels in my corner, I know things will always work out. When it came time to walk down the aisle, the sun came out and stayed with us for the rest of the evening. The dragonflies joined us, flying around in the most incredible patterns. To be honest, the whole thing felt completely magical and perfect, and I know Erin was right there with me. I have a lot to be thankful for. I know how fortunate I am to find so much love and incredible energy not once, but twice in a lifetime.

After fourteen years in the sport, I still play roller derby and wonder if it's because it keeps me connected to Erin. I play with a whole new generation of skaters who never had the privilege to meet her, but I do my best to keep her memory alive. I'm surrounded by the most supportive and dedicated teammates, and I know Erin would be so proud of and happy for all of us. As we go on adventures and make new memories to cherish, I always wish Erin was here with us. I envision a world in which she knows how much of an influence she has on those in the sport, its players, and beyond.

The loss of Erin will stay with so many of us forever. I can't fathom the hurt, sadness, and pain my best friend was in that led to the finality of that day, but I carry the lessons I learned into all my interactions. I will work to keep Erin's memory alive, I will celebrate her life, and I will forever be her voice.

Life is hard, and we will all encounter obstacles that may seem impossible to overcome. We will all suffer loss and heartbreak. In the midst of this, small acts of support and kindness go a long way. I will always hear Erin's voice saying, "You got this," and I'll keep pressing forward and reminding others that they're not alone.

I love you Erin. Thank you for all that you taught us and for the memories we shared. I will use your story to help others, and I will love with no conditions. Until we meet again, I will forever be loving you, #74.

They say it takes a village to raise a child. Doreen Coady has devoted her life to that concept, having seen proof of concept in her own son, Michael. His success in life, despite a condition called quadriplegia, earned Doreen a place among parenting greats. Now an empty-nester, Doreen is a motivational speaker and mentor prompting her parenting style and the heaps of wisdom she's compiled over the years. She has gathered 2,000 tips from 200 parents to give everyone a village. Her mission is to help communities and parents raise caring, resilient, and (most importantly) happy adults.

# VICTORY OVER VILE

## By Doreen Coady

I am an imposter!

I'm living a beautiful life, full of love and abundance. I smile. I'm grateful, hardworking, and happy. To the untrained eye, I have it all. I have it all. I have everything I ever wanted and more than I dreamed; yet it does not feel true. *Who the hell do I think I am anyway?*

The words of my vile, drunk and distant father ricochet in my mind as I continue to fight for my right to live and to be: Who the fuck do you think you are?

I ache to achieve, grow, love and learn. I'm in a war with accepting my happiness while my mind is in constant battle. Questioning my value was the only paternal engagement I had. Aren't they supposed to help, not only question? Don't parents have the answers?

Who the fuck do I think I am? The one question I'm still unable to answer after almost five decades.

I've calculated over 10,000 hours of seeking and personal development. The Gladwell rule says that makes me an expert, a master. I'm elite, an outlier. I'm in the dark, a six-year-old with a PhD. I dress like a professional, yet feel like an orphan. I am an orphan.

For almost fifty years, with over 10,000 hours of personal development, his voice still booms. It echoes. His disdain for me and for the world overpowers my valiant and ambitious efforts. Am I losing or winning? Despite him, I achieve. I smile. I accomplish. I grow. I continue.

I'm sad, afraid, and riddled with anxiety. It isn't apparent to everyone. It isn't apparent to anyone. Although I've shared the weight of it all, my lipstick and earrings fool the world. I am heavy. My head and heart are like lead. My breath, my movements, are laborious. I'm alone, yet surrounded by love. I've found food, shelter, affection, and hope. I seek understanding. The damage is deep and dismal, yet I march with confidence and purpose. At times I feel the end will be welcomed as the burden is great.

A dark, dingy basement with a pack of smokes and box of cheap wine is my fate. I consciously resist it with every day that I leave my home. Some days I don't leave. Loneliness calls, always. The urge to push others away and hide exactly "who the fuck I think I am" permeates my soul. My fear and discontent are his legacy and my heritage. That asshole!

God this makes me sad.

The bright side, even with the heaviness of a heartache, I have it all. I remain. I have accomplished everything—my wildest dreams, even. I did it. My first goal was achieved at sixteen years old when I got my driver's license. I knew then that I could *do* something. I had an identity and identification. This was who I was. I was no longer just "a fucking idiot." I was now a driver, a licensed, *bona fide* driver. I had something, my first something. Luckily for the public my family now had a sober driver. Luckily for me I had hope.

I went straight up from there. My next goal: Get the hell out of that house. That goal was also realized at sixteen. I left and never slept there again. I was free. Homeless and happier than ever. Freedom remains my most cherished value.

Martin Luther King said it best, "There is nothing in all the world greater than freedom. It's worth paying for it; it's going to jail for. I would rather be a free pauper than a rich slave. I would rather die in abject poverty than live in inordinate riches with the lack of self-respect."

I had self-respect. In my home, a 'self' was not permitted. Self-respect was never introduced; however, I had found it.

I vividly remember my first autumn in this great new world. I can still feel the cool air, smell the leaves even. Truly, it's as though I had never noticed leaves before with their colour and their crispness. I was Alice in my own Wonderland.

My goals continued. I graduated from high school, albeit homeless. I worked at a day care for an hour a day, thirty minutes before school and thirty minutes following. I made twenty dollars per week. I walked from wherever I landed to get there, not knowing where the day would lead. I felt like a failure, yet also that I was succeeding every day.

With the kindness of parents and the sympathies of teachers, I crossed the stage. I stole my graduation dress and borrowed my prom dress, all the while feeling like a loser even on the day of my greatest victory.

Now I had to find a way to sustain myself. Welfare was my only option and therefore my next goal. I was advised by my government that I did not qualify for financial aid, despite being homeless and broken; however, they said, "If you had a child, we would be concerned with their well-being."

"You're telling me if I had a kid I could get a cheque?" I asked. The heartless man confirmed what had been said and I replied, "See you in nine months."

My next goal was accomplished. Pregnant and on welfare, I had the rent. I had also found love and purpose.

My goals grew, as did my ambition. I wanted to be a great mom, not a mediocre mom. I wanted to be able to afford food, milk, and gas all at the same time. I wanted the best for him. I was a mom. I had an identity. No longer was I just a licensed driver, I was a mom. I again ached for freedom. Tied to the government and confined by their restrictions, I planned. I was mobilized. I sought and I found.

My life goal and my career ambition to be a receptionist, which was once thought to be unattainable, was realized. My dream was to work a front desk, to dress up and to have 'clicky shoes.' I didn't think I could ever achieve that. The Women's Center gave me clothing and I stole whatever else I needed. A new piece of my identity formed; I was now a professional. Dressed as a secretary, but a thief underneath, I was still an imposter. As I painted my face each day the question, "Who the hell do you think you are?" dampened any enthusiasm I could muster. So many goals achieved, yet I still considered myself a fake, a failure, and a fraud. That's who I thought I was. Had I given my father that answer when he'd asked me, I'm sure I would have affirmed my darkest belief.

I would have for once been validated. My son's bright eyes lifted me higher. He didn't think I was a "fucking idiot."

I wanted more. I wanted winter tires, plush towels, a medical plan, and a university education. I wanted him to have a mom to be proud of—more than anything, ever. I grabbed my machete and cleared his path.

Education, check. Tires, check. Towels, check (not yet plush or large, but check). Next goal: a meaningful career, check. Medical plan, check. My son's approval, check, check, check. Then, an unexpected outcome—I found love.

After twenty-three years of disapproval and disappointment, I found someone who loved me. I needed him to never ask, "Who the hell do you think you are?" He never did. I also needed him to never know who the hell I thought I was. I still need those things.

As an imposter I acted as if I had self-respect and value. I acted as if I had confidence and certainty. I acted as if I mattered and was worthy of love. I upheld standards while fearing each expectation would scare my love away. Nothing did.

Next set of goals: Safety and security. Check, check. Although accomplished, I remained afraid of knowing who I was. I held an intense fear others would uncover my secret and learn who I was. I acted normally, but I was so damaged and fear-filled. My lipstick hid my anxiety and my heels hid my broken heart. They still do.

Together we built a safe, secure, and loving home in which I felt unsafe, insecure, and unlovable. With a home full of smiles and a heart full of hurt, I marched on.

Dreams developed into goals. I got better towels, stronger love, and had milk and gas every week. All of these were once thought to be elaborate and ostentatious ambitions. I quit smoking and addressed both my physical and mental health. Things grew. I felt like a fraud. I still do.

We travelled. We hit Disney, Jamaica, Cuba, Dominican, Mexico, and even Dubai. My dreams were unyielding. I found my leaders: Oprah, Tony Robbins, Barack Obama. I shared space with them, learned from them, adding to my already 10,000 hours of personal development. I continued to develop while feeling like I didn't belong. I'm exhausted. I'm elated. I received a pardon yet still felt like a criminal. My government forgave me, yet I could not. My father would never forgive me. Such power, such pain. I wonder who he wanted me to be. I still do.

I've found a love like no other, a life I never imagined and lived magical experiences. I still felt fictitious, even though I had accomplished every dream and goal.

The earned and deserved respect of family, friends, and colleagues felt fragile. As a kind, caring, compassionate person with integrity, I guarded an internal mess, a secret question that remained in my core. After all was said and all was done, I was not able to answer "Who the hell do I think I am?" I am still pulled to the reclusive life of a lonely basement dweller. I have not yet succumbed.

I will continue to dream and do. I will at times be elated and others exhausted. I will feel deserving and still feel despair. I will feel like an imposter, but not always. Both things can be true.

I wish my father had told me who I was, who he wanted me to be or what he meant. I like who the hell I think I am, but not always how the hell I feel.

I am successful. I am a great mother! I am an author. I am a non-smoker. I am healing. I am strong. I am resilient. I have large plush towels. I don't steal. I am loyal. I am hard-working. I earn my way. I am loved. I matter. I get shit done.

That's who I am.

Made in the USA
Monee, IL
24 June 2021